INTO THE
PRIMITIVE

Into The Primitive

Advanced Trapping Techniques

DALE MARTIN

PALADIN PRESS
BOULDER, COLORADO

Also by Dale Martin:
The Trapper's Bible

Into the Primitive:
Advanced Trapping Techniques
by Dale Martin

Copyright © 1989 by Dale Martin

ISBN 13: 978-0-87364-530-0
Printed in the United States of America

Published by Paladin Press, a division of
Paladin Enterprises, Inc.
Gunbarrel Tech Center
7077 Winchester Circle
Boulder, Colorado 80301 USA
+1.303.443.7250

Direct inquiries and/or orders to the above address.

PALADIN, PALADIN PRESS, and the "horse head" design
are trademarks belonging to Paladin Enterprises and
registered in United States Patent and Trademark Office.

Visit our website at www.paladin-press.com.

CONTENTS

PREFACE
ix

CHAPTER ONE
Food
1

CHAPTER TWO
Water and Fire
71

CHAPTER THREE
Shelter
89

CHAPTER FOUR
Around the Camp
101

CHAPTER FIVE
Path Guarders, Alarms, and Weapons
121

AFTERWORD
165

PREFACE

My best camping buddy, who is also my brother, has made this statement to me a number of times: "I only need two things to survive in the wilderness. A Bowie knife and a $20,000 fully stocked camping trailer!" I still laugh every time he says it.

I have to admit that I will always use the modern conveniences as long as they are available, even when roughing it. But I have always found primitive trapping, camping, hunting, and fishing an interesting subject. I enjoy learning about the old ways and experimenting with them.

This book is centered around the concept of having ideas in mind about survival, just in case you actually have to use them at some point. Stranded. Alone. Or even, in a worst-case scenario, pursued by an aggressive enemy.

This text is not a "fight-back" book. There are enough of those around. Eighty percent of this book deals with primitive techniques in the following areas: water gathering, food gathering, snaring, trapping, shelter, fishing, and camping. The 20 percent of this book that does deal with primitive weapons and man traps is presented to show you how to slow down an aggressor and escape, rather than how to be on the offensive. Some of the traps and weapons described are quite dangerous, and should never be used except in an effort to save your own life.

If you are interested in the old ways and are "into the primitive," I hope you will enjoy this book.

CHAPTER ONE

Food

Food is generally not a survival problem when you are stranded in the wilds. Sounds crazy, doesn't it? But, in some situations, it has some truth. If you are going to be able to walk out or be rescued in a few days, you won't die of starvation, provided you can find water. And if you have no equipment at all, you might expend more energy catching the food than it would be worth.

However, given a knife, a few rudimentary scrounge-able materials, and knowledge of some food-gathering techniques, you can make a short or extended stay in the wilderness more comfortable.

There are many variables in the search for food in the wild. One of these is your location. If you are in Death Valley, for example, the first section of this chapter on fish gathering is not going to do you a great deal of good. But, in large areas of the United States, there will be a pond, lake, or stream within a mile in almost any direction.

Another unknown factor is the type of materials you will be able to scrounge up when the time arrives for you to put the knowledge in this book to use. So, my intent is to show a lot of different methods and items and let the reader cull out what he cannot use at the time.

FISH-GATHERING TECHNIQUES

Given a survival situation, if I were in an area that had even a small stock pond with small perch in it and all I had was a pocketknife, fish would be the first order of business.

Why? Because fish are by far the easiest animal to catch in quantities large enough to feed you (and possibly a fair-sized party), even with primitive equipment. Catching enough fish to last for a day or two will give you time to explore other food-gathering techniques.

The first thing you need to do is get all the ideas of traditional fishing out of your head. It doesn't matter at all if the fish you are eating are only an inch long if you are hungry. You're not planning on mounting them on your den wall, after all. And it doesn't matter if it is a "sport" fish. If you are hungry enough, a goldfish will taste great. And last but not least, slowly angling the fish to shore to give it a "fighting chance" and being a "sportsman" is all well and good if you are well fed. If you're not, you will be more interested in getting the fish any way you can.

Hollow-Log Trap

Hollow-log traps require little in the way of modern equipment—no hooks, no weights, no corks. They do require you to find:

1. A hollow log that is not too big for you to carry to the water. Actually, it doesn't even have to be a log. Any tube-like hollow cylinder of at least four inches but not

over twelve inches inside diameter will work. As long as it will readily sink to the bottom, it will probably work.

2. Something with which to plug up one end of the log. It doesn't have to be a solid tight plug; wire mesh would be fine. If no modern material such as wire mesh is available, find a rock that will go in one end of the log but won't fall out the other and will at least partially stop it up. Or you can block the end with sticks cut and lodged in the hole. If you have nails and string, you can weave a mesh like that on a cane-bottom chair to cover the end. All you are looking for is something to keep a fair-sized fish from getting out that end. Don't worry about the open end for now.

3. A rope or similar material of appropriate length with which to lower the log trap to the bottom of the water. Again, if no rope or stout cord is available, find a vine or some fibrous material. If you are stranded via a downed aircraft or disabled car, there will be plenty of electrical wire and cable in either to handle this job easily. It doesn't have to be pretty.

After closing off one end of the log, tie the rope (or vine, wire, or cable) around the other end so that when you lift up on the rope, the open end comes up first. See Figure 1 for details.

Throughout the South, and perhaps elsewhere, the hollow-log trap is used to catch catfish, *large* catfish. It works great for this, but it will work for lots of other fish, and fairly well for turtles, and (I know you wanted to hear this) even snakes.

Why fish go into the hollow-log trap is a mystery to me. I have heard a lot of different ideas about why this trap works, and the two main theories seem to be these:

The first is that when a fish swims into the end of the hollow log, he can't get out if the area is too small for him to turn around in, because some fish can't swim backward. Maybe this is true, but I can't swear to it.

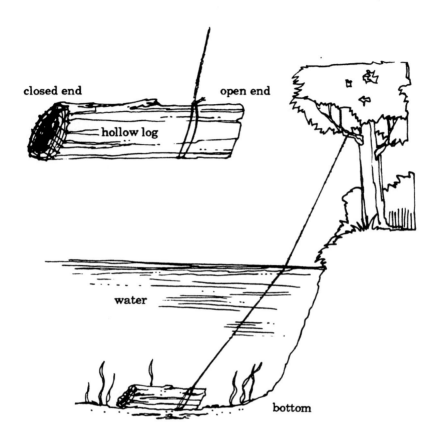

Figure 1. Hollow-Log Trap.

The second theory is that some species of fish (such as catfish) like to bury themselves in the bottom silt at times and just rest there—to den up, so to speak. A hollow log at the bottom of a lake or river is a convenient spot.

Regardless, the hollow-log trap does work well. Leave it on the bottom for several hours while you are fishing on your own using some of the other techniques in the book. Fish are not going to fight to see which can be the first to get in the trap, so it only needs to be checked every three or four hours. It requires no bait.

When checking the trap, pull up quickly on the rope so that the open end will be pulled up first and anything on the inside will not be able to get out.

Crayfish Trap

Do you like shrimp? Crayfish are almost the same thing, except they are freshwater critters. We used this trap as kids, predominantly in play. When we caught crayfish, we either threw them back or used them for fish bait. We didn't eat them. A good batch would be mighty welcome, however, given a hunger situation.

The trap is very simple and much like the hollow-log trap, only much smaller. It requires some string, a tin can, and some bait.

Poke two holes in the tin can on each side at the top to attach the string. Drive lots of holes in the side and especially in the bottom of the tin can. Put the bait in the can and lower it to the bottom. Lower slowly so the bait won't come out the top of the can. Obviously, the bait cannot be something that floats.

As with the hollow-log trap, leave the crayfish trap in the water for an hour or three and then pull it up. A good catch might only be eight or ten crayfish at a time, but every little bit helps, especially if you set six or eight of these cans.

A refinement you can use, if the materials can be found, is to fit a piece of screen wire (or some such material) over the bait in the bottom of the can. This serves two purposes. It keeps the bait from floating out if you lower the can to the bottom too quickly, and the crayfish tend to get their claws hung up in the screen wire, thus holding them until you pull the can up. See Figure 2.

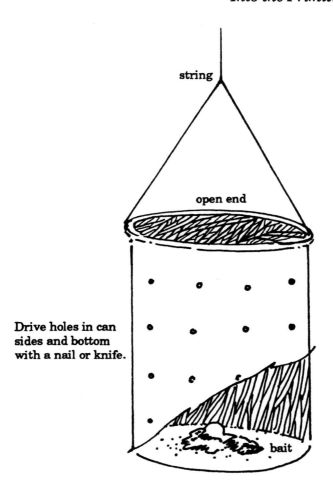

Figure 2. Crayfish Can Trap.

Bait

There is a variety of bait you can use for this trap and other traps. You might find yourself in a situation in which you can find materials for a trap, but you have no bait. As kids, we used bread. Given a survival situation, however, if you had bread, you would eat it.

Later in this book, you will see how to make primitive spears to catch fish, and several other methods to catch small fish with no bait. Besides using these techniques to catch fish for food, you can use them to get bait. Even a small perch cut into pieces makes a surprising amount of bait for a larger fish.

Not all bait is found in the water. Look in the trees and grass for insects to use. Grasshoppers are great, as are various caterpillars. You could dig for worms. Do you see any old decaying logs around? Odds are that if you can break up some rotting logs, you will find lots of large wood beetles inside. Spear a snake if you get the chance. A cut-up snake will provide lots of bait. Look for vultures — cut-up carrion is a good source of bait, too.

Suppose you had a .22 rifle. Shoot a bird (or whatever) and use the entrails for bait, or all of it if the rest of the bird is inedible. And while we're talking about .22s, a .22 shell shot into the ground and then dug up makes a good fishing weight, if you can spare the ammunition. Split it about halfway with your knife and clamp it onto the fishing line.

Suppose you had a hook and line, but no other equipment or bait. I've picked small (smaller than a shirt button), bright yellow flowers and used them on a hook to catch bait perch. Remember, you only have to catch one with the flower, because you can cut up the fish and have a fair amount of bait to catch more fish. Waste nothing — use whatever you have to get more.

Shallow-Pool Trap

This particular trap requires a specific geographic condition to be present at the lake or pond, but most people who have spent much time outdoors have seen the following situation.

Look for a small finger of water sticking out from the main body. The finger should only be a few feet wide (at most) and a few inches deep. The shallow pool cannot be so large that the fish can't be easily caught or speared once trapped there.

Close the narrow opening at the finger to about six inches wide by placing rocks in the water, forming a "fence" and "gate." This trap is less work if the gate area is only three or four inches deep and only a couple of feet wide. Generally speaking, however, the deeper and wider the gate, the bigger the catch. See Figure 3.

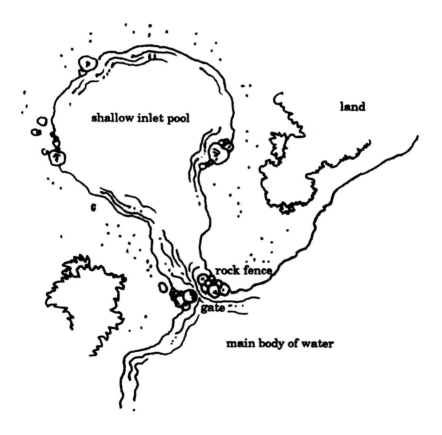

Figure 3. Shallow-Pool Trap.

Later, any fish caught in the shallow inlet pool can be taken by closing off the gate with a rock or rocks and then spearing or catching the fish with your hands. You might be able to trap some fish in the pool while you are building the fence and gate if you can approach from the right direction and keep them scared at the other side of the shallow pool while you fence them in. I'm never that lucky, but it is possible.

Usually, however, you will have to let the trap sit for an hour or three. When you come back to check it, approach from the direction least likely to scare the fish out of the gate. Wade in the water if necessary, and seal the gate with rocks. You probably will not catch any large fish in this type of trap. Small fish (this works great on small perch) swim around almost constantly, however, and will readily swim into these little inlets. Sometimes they even get trapped there when the water recedes naturally.

After several hours, if there are still no small fish in the trap, you may have to bait it with whatever you can chop up and chuck in. Insects, snakes, and turtles all make good bait when cut up, as do the bait sources we discussed earlier—the bloodier, the better.

Improvised Spears and Hooks

Suppose your tools are limited and you don't have any modern fishing spears or hooks. Primitive equipment can be improvised if you at least have a pocketknife and are good at scrounging.

Is there any bamboo or cane in the area? It is good for making a spear or gig for fish, frogs, and snakes. Figure 4 shows three gigs that are simple and easy to make if the materials are available.

Spear 1: Cut a length of cane or bamboo about six to eight feet long and at least three-quarters of an inch in diameter to be rigid enough to use as a spear. Cut off

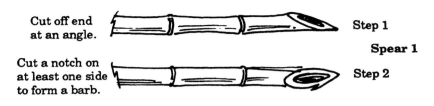

Cut off end
at an angle.   Step 1

                                                    Spear 1

Cut a notch on
at least one side   Step 2
to form a barb.

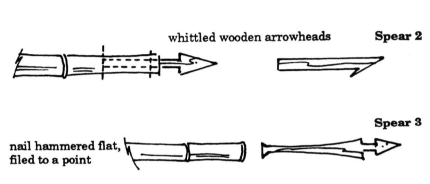

                    whittled wooden arrowheads   **Spear 2**

                                                    Spear 3

nail hammered flat,
filed to a point

Figure 4. Spears 1, 2, and 3.

the pointed end of the bamboo at an angle so that it is
reasonably sharp. Next, cut a notch on both sides of the
sharpened end (one side will suffice) to form something
similar to an arrowhead. The exact shape is not all that
important, but you want a barb with enough angle so
that your catch can't slide back off after it is speared.

Spear 2: Cut off the end of the bamboo spear evenly,
not at an angle. Then carve a wooden arrowhead to fit
in the end of it. Again, the shape of the head is not all
that important, as long as you have a barb on it.

You can secure the arrowhead in the end of the
bamboo by a couple of means. You should carve the
arrowhead shaft so it is a tight fit inside the bamboo.
You can glue it in if plant-resin glue can be obtained.
Pine-tree or sweet-gum sap makes adequate glue for
this. You can obtain some by wounding the side of a tree
with your knife or axe and letting the sap flow. The

second, and perhaps best method, is to slice away from one-third to one-half of the bamboo around the arrowhead shaft, exposing the shaft of the arrowhead on one side. You can then bind the shaft into the bamboo by lashing it *tightly* at that point. To be effective, the binding must have a good grip on the arrowhead shaft, as well as on the bamboo.

Sear the wooden arrowhead in your campfire to harden it. Also, make the arrowhead long enough so that when it dulls you can sharpen it several times before you have to replace it.

Important: When using this type of spear, no matter how securely you think the point is lodged in the end of the bamboo, pull it back carefully after spearing something against a riverbank. This will help keep the head from pulling out. Be easy with it—this is makeshift equipment.

Spear 3: Spear 3 is the same as Spear 2 except you use a nail (or something similar—look around) in the end of the spear. Many things might work, as long as you can file a barb on them. Attach and use as in Spear 2 instructions.

Spear 4: No bamboo or cane available? Find a sapling of the same size as we discussed for the bamboo spears. Whittle a couple of wooden heads as shown in Figure 5. Or you could use nails hammered flat and filed to an arrow shape. Cut slots on each side of the shaft to receive the points, and bind them tightly to the shaft of your spear. Even though the points are tied in, some of the tree-sap glue we talked about earlier wouldn't hurt here. Use the resin both under and over the binding.

Spear 5: Is there a barbed-wire fence in your area? If so, you may be able to make a "frog-gig" point out of barbed wire. *May* is the key word in the last sentence. If the barbed wire is the cheap imported kind, it probably won't work. Also, if you try to make the points that ex-

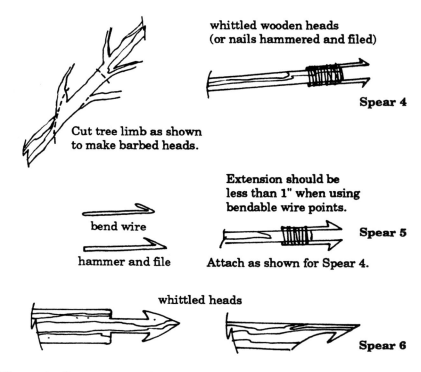

whittled wooden heads
(or nails hammered and filed)

Spear 4

Cut tree limb as shown
to make barbed heads.

Extension should be
less than 1" when using
bendable wire points.

bend wire

Spear 5

hammer and file

Attach as shown for Spear 4.

whittled heads

Spear 6

Figure 5. Spears 4, 5, and 6.

tend past the shaft more than an inch long, it probably won't be stiff enough, even if it is domestic wire. Keep the point short, as shown in Figure 5. Follow the same procedures as you did to make Spear 4, but use the wire points.

Spear 6: You have nothing but a pocketknife? Carve the end of the spear in a barbed fashion. Leave the shaped point long enough so you can sharpen it several times as needed before it is all whittled away. See Figure 5.

The symmetry of limb growth is vastly different from species to species of tree. Look for a limb (or, more likely, the trunk of a small sapling) that looks like the

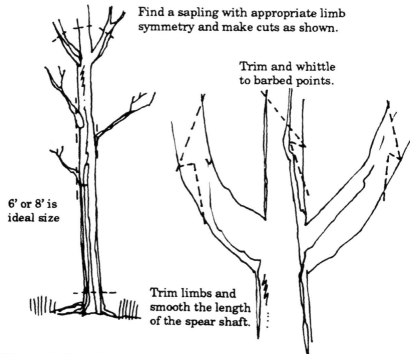

Find a sapling with appropriate limb symmetry and make cuts as shown.

Trim and whittle to barbed points.

6' or 8' is ideal size

Trim limbs and smooth the length of the spear shaft.

Figure 6. Spear 7.

one shown in Figure 6 and improvise. Spear 7 provides a three-prong spear, but is more time-consuming to make. See Figure 6 for the details of Spear 7.

Do you want a spear you can use over and over again? One with changeable heads? Find a limb or sapling of appropriate size and length and whittle the end of it in the style shown in Figure 7. Then you can make an extra head or two in case you break or lose one. See Figure 7 for details.

Improvised Hooks

Primitive hooks are a little tougher to make than

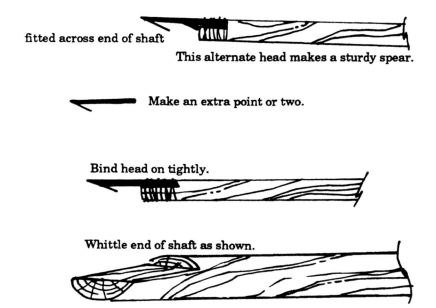

fitted across end of shaft

This alternate head makes a sturdy spear.

Make an extra point or two.

Bind head on tightly.

Whittle end of shaft as shown.

Figure 7. Spear 8.

spears. Small hooks work better—don't try to make a large one for a monster fish. As everyone knows, there is a heck of a lot more small (even tiny) fish to catch than large ones. Making small hooks requires a great deal of dexterity, however.

Hook 1: Do you have some basic tools like pliers and a file, but no modern fishhooks? If you can find some small but reasonably stiff wire, you can fashion your own. A coat hanger works well. A downed aircraft or disabled car will provide lots of stiff wire. Look around and use whatever is available.

This hook will not work as well as one that Eagle Claw makes. As a matter of fact, it won't even be remotely close. But it might keep you fed, with a little effort on your part. The details are shown in Figure 8.

Step 1   Step 2   Step 3

Bend the wire into a   Flatten the   File to barbed point.
hook, leaving an eyelet.   point area only.

Figure 8. Hook 1.

The hook's barb can be filed on backward (facing out) if necessary. It will not work as well, but is easier to make.

Hook 2: No wire around, but you have found a loose nail? This hook is the same as Hook 1, except it is made from a nail and does not have an eyelet to attach to the fishing line. The nail has to have a head on it; avoid headless or finish nails. The line is secured tightly under the head. See Figure 9 for details.

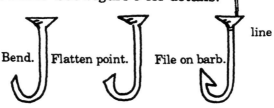

line

Bend.   Flatten point.   File on barb.

Figure 9. Hook 2.

The hooks shown in Figures 10 and 11 will only work once in about every twenty or thirty attempts—a very low percentage. However, if you are hungry enough, and there is not much around in the way of materials, give these a shot.

Hook 3: Find a very small tree limb with symmetry as shown in Figure 10. Make the cuts as shown, and carve the head to make a barb.

Hook 4: Are there any thornbushes around? Use them in much the same manner as in Hook 3. See Figure 11 for examples of these hooks.

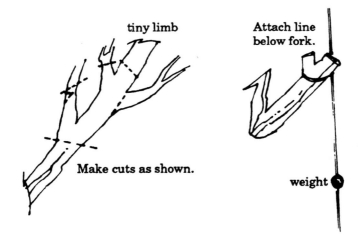

Figure 10. Hook 3.

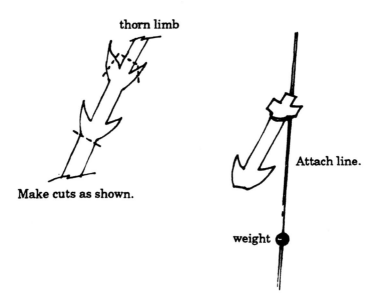

Figure 11. Hook 4.

Fishing-Pole Seine

This is a lazy man's little fish catcher. Commercially made models of this item are available, but you can make one yourself if you can scare up a few items. Most people use the commercially made models to catch minnows, but these homemade traps can catch small fish in the two- to three-inch category. See Figure 12.

First, cut a pole about the size of a standard cane fishing pole (or slightly larger). Don't use cane or bamboo, however. Use a solid pole.

Next, scrounge up some stiff wire. Coat-hanger wire is not really stiff enough, but it might have to do if nothing else is available. Try to find something a little more rigid, if possible.

Bend the wire into a square. Ideally, this square needs to be three feet or so on each side, but the wire you are able to obtain (and the size of the net to be placed inside the wire) may dictate the final size. Do the best you can. The wire needs to be all in one piece and wired together at only one of the four corners.

Next, cover the square of wire with some type of cloth. White seems to work best, but I don't know why. Got an old shirt? Sew the cloth onto the frame if you are lucky enough to have sewing materials. If not, tie it to the wire in several places along each side of the frame. Spread the cloth tightly across the square. You don't need much slack. You certainly don't want anything resembling a butterfly net.

Then, attach equal lengths of fishing line or some such cord to the four corners. Attach the other end of these four lines to *one* cord which will run up to the pole you made earlier.

Make a "Y" stake (or find a convenient limb on a tree) where you want to set the fishing-pole seine. Lash the pole *loosely* to it so the end with the seine on it is slightly heavier than the other end and hangs down.

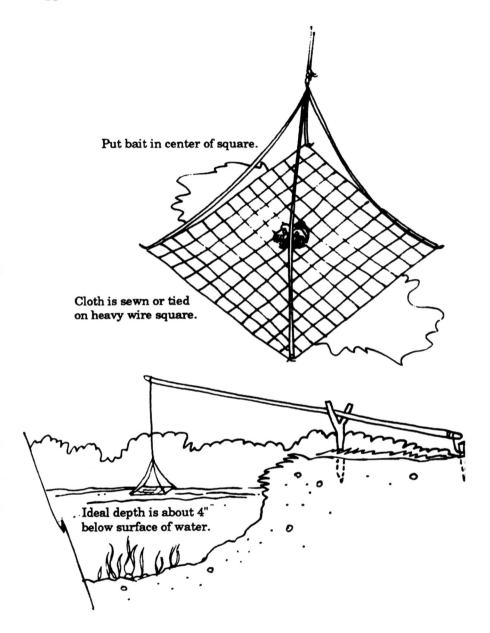

Put bait in center of square.

Cloth is sewn or tied
on heavy wire square.

Ideal depth is about 4"
below surface of water.

Figure 12. Fishing-Pole Seine.

Tie a cord to the other end of the pole, and run it down to a stake driven into the ground. In this way, you can tie the cord to a point that will hold the seine under the water at the desired depth. Wrap the cord around the pole so that you can adjust the depth of the seine in the water by the number of wraps.

Place a small amount of bait in the center of the cloth and lower the seine into the water about four to six inches. Tie the net to the stake with the cord.

Wait until some small fish swim over the top of the seine to get the bait lying on the cloth. Then, push down on the staked end of the pole quickly, which will pull up the seine end. Usually, if there are eight or ten small fish gathered to feed on top of the cloth, you will only catch about half of them, as the ones near the edge of the square will get away when you pull up the net. The trap can be used over and over, however, and might keep you alive, depending on the fish population.

Cloverleaf Fish Trap

Let's imagine a different situation. In this scenario, you have some basic tools (pliers, knife, and so on), a little bait, and you also have some wire screen available. Let us further suppose that you have managed to supply yourself to the point that being hungry is at least several days in the future, and what you would like to do is extend that "hungry point" even further into the future. Good, you've got it made. All you have to do is build a trap or two, and you will have something that will provide you with fish day after day with almost no effort on your part. See Figure 13.

The type of wire most often used for the cloverleaf fish trap is hardware cloth, which is galvanized steel wire screen. It comes in various widths, and the most common mesh sizes are quarter inch and half inch. It comes in a roll, like chicken wire, but you can usually

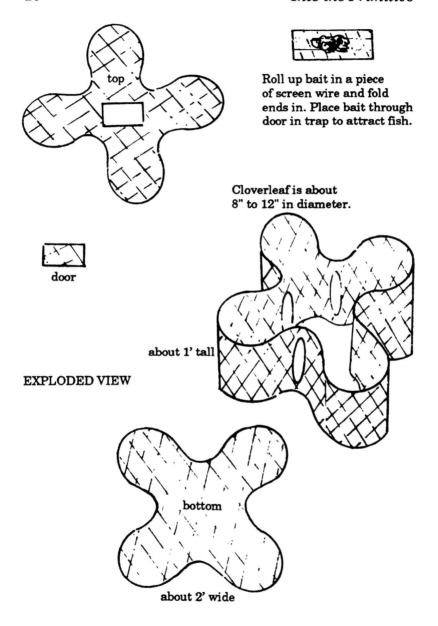

top

Roll up bait in a piece
of screen wire and fold
ends in. Place bait through
door in trap to attract fish.

Cloverleaf is about
8" to 12" in diameter.

door

about 1' tall

EXPLODED VIEW

bottom

about 2' wide

Figure 13. Cloverleaf Fish Trap.

buy a small piece of it at lumberyards or hardware stores.

You make one of these traps for a bait catcher to use at some future date, and buy the materials at a store rather than scrounging around. It doesn't matter much which mesh size you use; buy the larger half-inch mesh if you can, since it's cheaper. If you are scrounging for materials, other kinds of wire mesh work also, as long as it is about two feet wide and about ten feet long. Ideally, it needs to be fairly stiff wire that retains its shape, but yet is bendable and has mesh of less than one inch. Half inch or three-quarter inch is best.

Make the center cloverleaf structure first, then the top and bottom of the trap. This will ensure a better fit. Constructing the cloverleaf will be easier if you can find a round cylinder of appropriate size to form the mesh around; a roll of roofing felt is about the right size. Cut the wire as shown in the pattern in Figure 13, and wire the pieces together as implied in the exploded diagram.

Cut slits as shown in the cloverleaf, and bend the cut wire barbs inward. These slits are the four points by which the fish enter the trap. Make the slits about three-quarters inch wide and six inches tall. Finally, wire the door on the trap so that it can be used as an opening to add bait and remove fish.

This trap is the very best fish trap I have seen. I caught *literally thousands* of small fish in one of these traps over a period of a few days. This was done in an effort to rid a small lake of perch to give catfish we stocked the lake with a chance to become established. It was not done in a survival situation, but if the water you are fishing has a large population of small bait fish, this trap is a "getter." The theory behind the cloverleaf trap is that the fish, drawn by the bait, find it easy to swim in through the slits of the trap but virtually impossible to get out. It is only good for small fish (no larger than five inches or so) unless you make the trap unusually large. But, as we have noted before, there are many more little ones than big ones.

Cone Trap

Is the cloverleaf trap too much trouble? Do you have a little bait and the wire mesh to make a trap, but want to get a trap in the water quickly? Or do you have a piece of trap wire that is a little too small for a cloverleaf? The cone trap is a lot simpler to make and, although not nearly as effective, will still catch enough small fish to feed you. See Figure 14.

First, you need some wire mesh with the properties we discussed earlier for the cloverleaf trap. It needs to be reasonably stiff, but bendable. Hardware cloth is the most common type used for these traps, but other wire could be substituted.

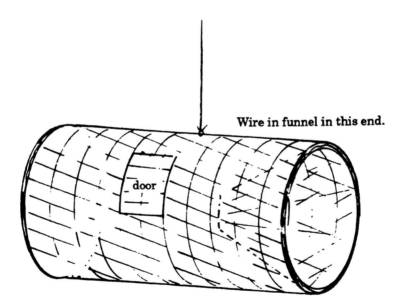

Figure 14. Funnel Trap.

The amount of mesh you need, however, is considerably less than that used in the cloverleaf trap. A piece about two feet by three feet will be enough to make this trap.

First, roll the wire into a cylinder about eight inches or so in diameter and open on both ends. Cut a door opening, as shown in Figure 14, that can be used to add bait and remove fish. Save enough wire mesh to cover one of the open ends and wire on the cover firmly. Make a funnel for the other end; if materials are available and the cylinder is long enough, you can put a funnel at both ends.

Wire the cylinder, the end, and the funnel together, as shown. Leave the funnel opening whatever size is appropriate for the fish you are seeking. Usually these traps are made with a one- to two-inch funnel opening for small fish, but could be made larger if materials are available.

After construction, put a small amount of bait inside the trap and lower it in the water. The bait can be folded up inside a piece of screen wire, if available, so it will last longer.

The theory behind the funnel trap is the same as the cloverleaf trap. Fish find it easy to swim *into* the funnel, but once inside, find it very difficult to get *out*.

Fish Bomb

Ever hear of GIs using hand grenades for fishing during wartime? They would chuck one into a likely spot, and it would have time to sink most of the way to the bottom of the water before it exploded. When it went off, the dead and stunned fish would float to the top.

The fish bomb works in the same manner. It would probably be very difficult to scrounge up all the materials and construct this device if you are stranded suddenly without the proper tools. If you have access to a workshop, however, keep this device in mind.

Find a flashlight bulb and break the glass without breaking the filament inside. This is easier said than done. Solder on two insulated wires at the normal contact points. Solder can be obtained from electrical connections on downed aircraft or disabled cars. Electrical wire can be obtained from the same sources. The difficult and tedious part of making this trap is the actual soldering by using matches (no soldering gun).

Cap one end of a short piece of pipe. Insert the filament with wires soldered onto the bottom. Pour gun powder into the pipe, covering the filament. *Important*: Use a funnel to pour the powder into the pipe, even if you have to make one with paper. The reason is you don't want to get any powder on the threads of the open end, because when you screw the cap on that end, powder on the threads might cause it to go off in your hands. This would ruin your whole day!

Another option is to use a small plastic bag to hold the powder and the filament inside the pipe. This might keep the powder dry a little longer in the event of a small leak, thus giving you time to detonate the device. In addition, you can fold the edges of the plastic bag over the end of the pipe to avoid getting powder on the pipe threads.

Drill a hole in another pipe cap to allow the two wires to pass through with as little extra room as possible. Run the wires through the cap, and screw the cap on. See Figure 15.

Take the two electrical wires and wrap, tie, or tape them to the shaft of the pipe. When the fish bomb is lowered into the water, it will be suspended from this point. The reason for doing this is to keep from pulling the filament out of the powder while lowering the device, and to keep from pulling on the wires where they come out of the pipe cap. *Warning:* if the caps are not screwed on well, water will leak inside; this opening

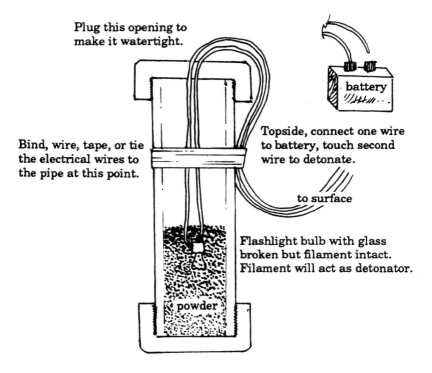

Plug this opening to make it watertight.

Bind, wire, tape, or tie the electrical wires to the pipe at this point.

battery

Topside, connect one wire to battery, touch second wire to detonate.

to surface

Flashlight bulb with glass broken but filament intact. Filament will act as detonator.

powder

Figure 15. Fish Bomb.

where the wires come out will have to be plugged. Plug the wire hole with waterproof glue, melted wax, solder, tree resin, or some such material. It must be watertight.

You are now ready to lower the fish bomb into the water (as deep as possible—at least several feet, depending upon how much powder you inserted). You detonate the device by connecting a flashlight battery to the two wires leading from the device. When you touch the second wire to the battery terminal after you've connected the first, the bomb will detonate, provided it has not leaked full of water or the filament has not been damaged.

If it doesn't go off, don't be an idiot and pull it up to see what's wrong. Leave it on the bottom and go on to something else. For that matter, use a fish bomb only if there are no other alternatives. Be careful!

Trotlines and Setlines

Trotlines and setlines are so common in the South that everyone knows what they are and how they are used. However, not everyone lives in the South, so we will go over them briefly.

A trotline is feasible if you have some line and modern hooks and want to set a large number of hooks in the water to continually bring in fish. A trotline is one line (usually fifty feet or more) with a number of hooks (usually twenty-five to fifty) attached at about three-foot intervals. The hooks are actually attached to smaller lines about a foot long, which are, in turn, attached to the main line. The trotline is weighted and set in the water at whatever depth is appropriate for the fish you are trying to catch.

Setlines are simply single versions of a trotline. A setline is a hook on the end of a line that is hung either from a limb or from a pole stuck into the mud at the water's edge.

Both trotlines and setlines have advantages and drawbacks. Trotlines put a lot of hooks into the water at one time, but you normally have to have a boat to check them.

Setlines only put one hook in the water for each line set, but you can check them from the bank. Also, if you set them with poles, you can usually see the poles jiggle from a distance if there is anything on them. Some people even tie bells on them. Good luck!

ANIMAL-TRAPPING TECHNIQUES

I love snares, and I'm not quite sure why. It may be

because they are cheap and easy to make, or because they are generally hard to spot once set in the woods. But I think the real reasons are these: they are chillingly effective, they are primitive, and mastering snaring gives you a sense of being able to do something special, since snaring is becoming a lost art.

Snares are probably the oldest form of trapping. They have been used for untold centuries in Africa, and other parts of the world, yet most people have never seen one in real life. Those who have seen them in movies and TV often assume that they are one of those things that only work on television, and not in real life.

But snares *do* work extremely well. Their construction is simplicity itself, and they are cheap to make as well. What more could you ask for?

Small Snares

The first seven snares shown will be small ones for rabbit-size game. They might take a small fox, but it would definitely be chancy. Usually it takes a heavier line on a snare for anything bigger than rabbit-size game. For these snares, and their refinements, the same general type of wire can be used.

The first lesson in snaring is to *always use wire* for the snare lasso. Rope or cord does not work very well. There are reasons for this. First, when jerked taut, wire will cut into the prey somewhat and not loosen, thus trapping (or killing) the prey. Second, the right type of wire will almost hold itself upright and looped open without any support. Third, wire is difficult for a captive animal to chew through *if* it can get its teeth on it.

There are many different types of wire you can use. In addition to having the qualities discussed above, the wire you choose has to be of a reasonable thickness for the game you are seeking. Other than that, there are no specific requirements.

The small coils of picture-frame hanging wire that you can buy at the grocery store's hardware section will work well. Copper electrical wire stripped of the insulation makes the best snares I have ever seen. If you have access to a downed aircraft or disabled car, electrical wire can be salvaged from them. Look around.

The construction of small snare lassos is easy once you have the necessary wire. The following description assumes that you have located a source of copper electrical wire.

Secure a two-foot piece of 18-2 appliance wire. (You can use anything close to this; 16-2 would be fine, also.) This wire is common and cheap; a two-foot piece of this wire might cost fifty cents or less. Got an old extension cord with the insulation crumbling off? Use it; you'll have to peel the insulation off the copper wire anyway.

Once acquired, examine the wire. This type of wire has two halves, each with insulation covering an inner core of copper wire. Split the two halves of the insulated wire so that you now have two 2-inch pieces of wire with insulation still attached.

Next, using a pair of pliers and a knife to get it started, peel the insulation off the inner core of the soft fibers of copper wire on both pieces. There should be forty or fifty small hairlike strands of copper wire inside the insulation of each of the two-foot pieces, depending on what gauge wire you were able to obtain. Take care not to tangle up the copper strands as you peel off the insulation.

Divide the strands in each two-foot piece by half, again being careful not to tangle them. You should now have four 2-foot pieces of wire, with each piece having twenty to twenty-five strands in it. (If you used a scrounged piece of wire from an old lamp and it's of a size that you end up with a few less strands or a few more, don't worry about it. As few as fifteen strands will be okay for rabbit-size game, and as many as thirty won't be too many. I find, however, that twenty to twenty-five strands is about ideal.)

Now, take one of the four pieces you are working with and twist the wire slightly so it becomes more tightly woven into a single strand, rather than twenty to twenty-five strands of copper just lying together loosely. The final, more tightly woven single strand should be about the size of a pencil lead, maybe half again larger.

Next, evenly cut off the ends of the wire you are working with and twist the ends so they will not unravel easily. Now, follow the previous two steps on the other three pieces of wire you have. Note that out of one piece of two-foot-long 18-2 (or similar) lamp-cord wire, we end up with enough material to make four snares of this small size. How's that for economy?

Make a loop on each end of each piece of wire. Each loop should be about the size of a dime. One loop will serve as the connection to the spring-pole mechanism, and the other will form the lasso itself.

Run one loop through the other to form the snare lasso on the snare wire. Draw up the loop on the wire that forms the lasso so the wire has just enough room to slide through when put under tension. You should now have a wire snare with the lasso already formed as shown in Figure 16.

The next step is to locate a good tree to use as a spring pole. The spring pole is what jerks the line taut around the animal once the trigger is tripped. The small sapling you choose for a spring pole will have to be springy enough so that, if it is bent over, it will pop back up when released. This is a very important detail. Some small saplings, when bent over, will lose their tendency to pop back. You can usually tell by the feel of the return pull when you bend one over whether or not it will work. If you are undecided on a potential spring pole, bend it over several times. If it does not snap back

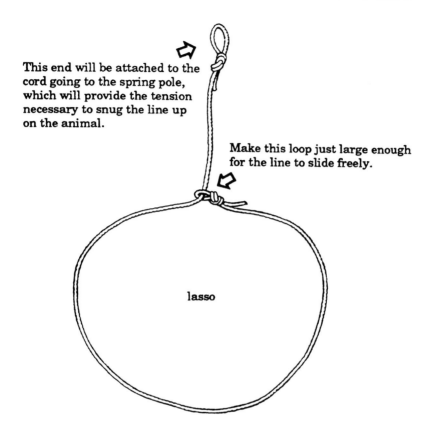

This end will be attached to the cord going to the spring pole, which will provide the tension necessary to snug the line up on the animal.

Make this loop just large enough for the line to slide freely.

lasso

Figure 16. Snare Lasso.

quickly to an upright position, it is not the right tree.

A good spring pole will dictate the location of the snare, as this is a baited trap and does not have to be on a trail or at the entrance to the animal's den.

Attach a piece of cord (I use fairly heavy trotline cord) to the tip of the spring pole. You will probably have to trim most of the limbs out of the way on the spring pole itself.

Pull down on the cord you have attached to the spring pole to where the pole is exerting enough pull to jerk a four- or five-pound weight off the ground if the cord were released suddenly.* Now, make sure the cord will reach to within an inch or so of the ground. Cut off any excess.

Next, whittle a peg from a tree branch to use as a trigger, as shown in Figure 17. You will also need to drive a stake into the ground with a nail in it as part of the trigger. For trigger details, see Figure 18.

Next, tie the wire snare to the cord going to the string pole, and set the trigger as shown in Figures 17 and 18. In studying these illustrations, it should be apparent that any slight tug on the snare lasso by an animal trying to get through it will bump the peg off the nail. Up will go the spring pole, tightening the wire lasso and catching the animal.

If necessary, use twigs, grass, or weeds to hold the snare in the desired position. Little else will be needed. Copper wire is small in diameter, pliable, and strong enough to hold the game once caught. The stiff nature of the wire will allow it to almost stand by itself—the loop will hold itself open and very little grass or weeds will be needed to hold it up. Once tripped, the cutting nature of the copper wire will keep it snubbed tight so the animal cannot get out.

Now, before we get too far down the line in snare setting, you need to decide why you are setting this snare. It will make a difference in how you continue.

One reason someone would set snares is for food—for simple survival or to supplement the family table. The other common reason for snare setting is for the hide. You might be interested in collecting the hide of fur-bearing animals, which can be sold to fur buyers for the

---

* If you set the spring pole with too much pull, it will be harder to trip the trigger. A little variance will not matter, but do not set the spring pole with the pull too strong. You can test the pull with a four- or five-pound weight tied to the end of the spring-pole cord.

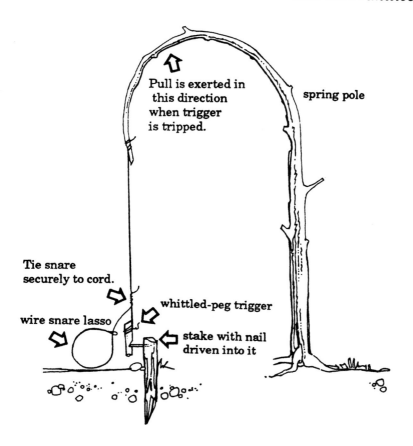

Pull is exerted in this direction when trigger is tripped.

spring pole

Tie snare securely to cord.

whittled-peg trigger

wire snare lasso

stake with nail driven into it

Figure 17.

good old American dollar.

In the first case, if you are in search of food, you want to set the snare so it will not kill the animal if at all possible. If you set a snare for rabbits (or whatever) and catch one in the first hour or two, by the time you come back the next morning to check the snare, the meat will be spoiled if the snare has killed the animal. Of course, this would not be a concern if you checked the set every hour or two, but usually you cannot check a set that often.

If you are merely selling hides and have no interest in the meat, you would probably *prefer* that the snare kills the animal, to reduce the chances that the animal will ruin the pelt in many hours of struggling against the snare.

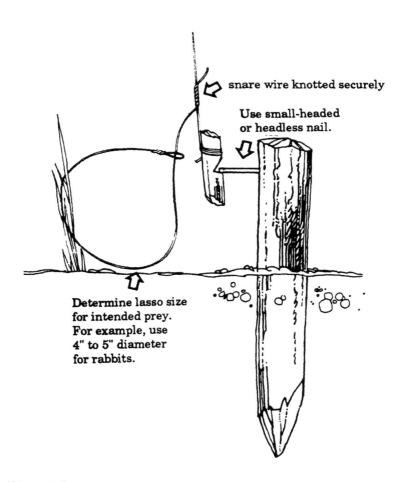

snare wire knotted securely

Use small-headed or headless nail.

Determine lasso size for intended prey. For example, use 4" to 5" diameter for rabbits.

Figure 18.

In each of the two instances listed, the snare is set *slightly* differently to bring about the desired result. It must be noted that there is no sure thing in setting snares. When you set a snare to kill the animal, sometimes it will not do so. Also, when you set a snare merely to hold an animal, sometimes the animal will die. Snares are primitive and cannot be completely controlled. What follows here will help you set them so they do what you want the majority of the time.

A change in the snare setting can be done with the spring pole. Assume that you are after food in a case of simple survival. The animal you are attempting to snare is in the four-pound range. Now, simple logic will tell you that the farther over you bend the spring pole when setting the trigger, the more force it is going to have jerking up when the trigger is released. Or, vice versa, if the pole is bent over only slightly during the set, its pull strength on the snared animal will not be nearly so great. Thus, the same spring pole can be set for a variety of pull strengths depending upon how far toward the ground you bend it in setting the snare.

So, in the example of snaring for simple survival food, set the pull strength of the spring pole so it will *not quite* pull a four-pound animal off the ground. The reason for this is that if the snare catches the prey directly on the throat and lifts the animal completely off the ground, it will die very quickly, and the meat will be spoiled if you do not get back to the snare within a fairly short period of time. Yet, at the same time, the spring pole needs to exert enough pull on the snare to keep the line snubbed tight around the animal.

In the second case, where you merely want the hide of the animal, set the spring pole so the four-pound animal will be held helpless in the air once caught. If the snare happens to catch the animal directly around the neck, it will kill it, but in this scenario you would not care.

In both cases, as stated before, the end result is not always perfect. In the "for food" case, sometimes the animal will die in your snare regardless of what you do. This will not happen often, but could happen at least part of the time.

In the second case, the snare *quite often* will not kill the animal. The animal may be killed if the snare catches the animal around the neck, but snares rarely do this. The animal is usually about halfway through or at least has one of its front legs through before the snare trips. However, if the snare is set so the animal is held off the ground, helpless in the air, it *will* still minimize the pelt destruction of a struggling animal.

Please note that if you are setting the snare for anything that comes along, this refinement will not apply. This technique works on the principle of knowing in advance the approximate size (weight) of the intended animal. If you are setting a snare in an area where it might catch a two-pound animal or a ten-pound animal with equal likelihood, you will just have to set the snare for an average size, and hope for the best.

Now, back to Figure 17. By now, in reading and studying the illustrations, it should be evident that an animal trying to pass through the lasso would probably spring the trigger and be caught. But, how do you get the animal to walk right into the trap?

Two ways. The first requires little explanation. You set the snare at the entrance to the animal's den hole so it will snare the animal in its natural comings and goings. The second way is done with bait.

There are probably a lot of good ideas floating around out there for setting snares with bait. The system I always use is this: using whatever is available (two-by-fours, sticks, logs, whatever), I build a "box canyon" on the ground with the bait at the closed end and the snare set at the open end. For example, if I am in the woods away from other materials, I can usually find a log like one you might use in a campfire. I pile up two or three such logs, usually a foot or so tall, put the bait in the boxed end, and cover the top to form a lid. This setup works almost as well without the top cover, but use the cover when materials are available. You can drive stakes into the ground, creating a small fence, to use in the same manner, but more work is involved. This whole setup sounds like a lot of work, and a hassle to find the materials, but it's really not. See Figure 19.

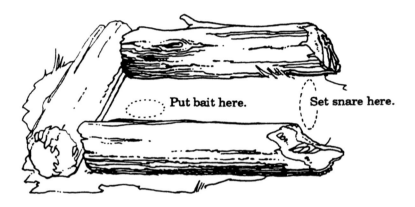

Figure 19. Box-Canyon Trap.

One last thing about these small snares: the two most variable items are the snare set location and the size of the wire. There are lots of other variations in snaring, but by varying these two factors, you can adapt this basic snare to a variety of game.

1. *Location.* If you are setting a snare for an animal that will come to bait, the box canyon will serve you well. It will force the animal to go through the snare to get to the bait. It works well on foxes, opossums, or raccoons. (It also works well on your neighbor's house cat, so be discreet if you set one of these in an urban area.) It allows you to set the snare under a good spring-pole

sapling since it does not have to be at the animal's den-hole entrance or some *specific* spot.

If, however, you are setting this snare without bait for an animal that doesn't come to bait readily (rabbits, for example), a good spot is usually at the entrance to the animal's den hole, where it will catch the animal in its natural comings and goings.

Other locations may work well in certain instances. Is a fox getting in your chicken house through a small hole in the fence? Set the snare at the hole and nail him. Animal trails can be used to advantage in the same way.

2. *Size of the wire.* This part is fairly obvious. The electrical wire described earlier for making a small snare would be good for rabbits or smaller animals. It might take something a little larger, but it might not.

For anything larger than a rabbit, up to the size of a raccoon, double, triple, or even quadruple the number of strands of copper fibers in your snare lasso. Use common sense. Obviously, the thicker the snare lasso wire, the larger the animal it will hold.

Later in this book, you will see how to use small cable for even larger game. But first, let's look at some similar small snares and some refinements of technique.

Small-Snare Variations

The next snare we will look at is identical to that discussed previously except for one factor: it uses no spring pole.

Consider this scenario. You have found a likely looking den-hole entrance. It might lead into a rabbit warren, or into a fox hole (you may be seeking hides rather than food). But, guess what? There is no sapling in sight to use as a spring pole. You have the snare lasso and the other materials, but there is no handy spring pole next to the den hole.

Look for a limb above you. If there is a tree nearby, it may be you can use the downward pull of a falling object to duplicate the upward jerk of a spring pole.

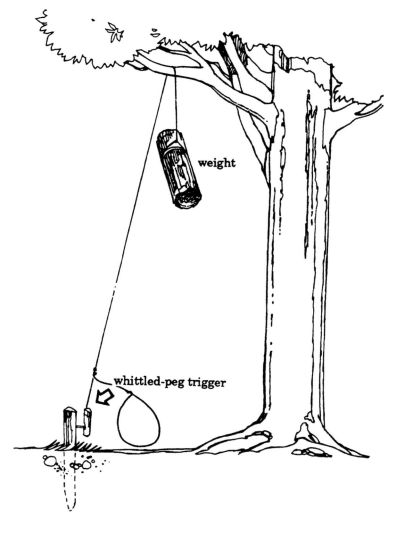

weight

whittled-peg trigger

Figure 20.

Set the snare exactly as before, but instead of tying the cord to a spring pole, run it over a limb above and tie a weight to it. Then, when the trigger is tripped, the weight falls, and the snare is jerked upward. If no tree limb is available, two long stakes driven in the ground and tied at the top, A-frame style, will accomplish the same thing. See Figure 20.

The amount of pull on this setup can be adjusted for various size animals, much the same as with the spring pole, by two factors: the amount of weight put on the end of the cord, and the height the weight is from the ground when set.

For example, let's say the animal you are after is a fox denned up in the bank of a creek bed, and there is a limb above that you can use to set the snare and weight. Let's estimate this fox to weigh ten pounds, and let's say you couldn't care less if it is stone dead when you come back to check the set because all you want is the hide anyway.

Set a twenty-pound weight about four feet off the ground. If the snare does not kill the fox outright, at least it will hold it helpless off the ground. In this position, even if still alive, the fox is less likely to damage its pelt in hours of struggling against the snare. It is also less likely to chew its way out of the snare in the air than if it were held on the ground.

Consider a second scenario. Same den hole. Same fox. Same tree limb with which to set the weighted snare. But in this example, you are going to check the snare every two hours. You are trying to catch the fox alive for sale to a game ranch.

In this case, you would set a ten-pound weight two feet off the ground. The pull of the weight won't kill the animal (usually) since it is approximately the same weight as the animal, and has only two feet to fall before hitting the ground. Yet it would be heavy enough so that it would be very difficult for the animal to pull the weight back over the limb and escape.

As with the spring pole, if you are setting the snare in a spot where catching a two-pound or a ten-pound animal is equally likely, this technique will not apply. It only works in cases where you are reasonably sure of the intended prey's size or weight.

Suppose you had no nail with which to set the trigger, but you did have the snare-wire lasso and the cord to use with a spring pole or weight. Fear not, all is not lost. Find a limb or sapling shaped as in Figure 21a. Cut and form the trigger stake, and set as shown in Figure 21b.

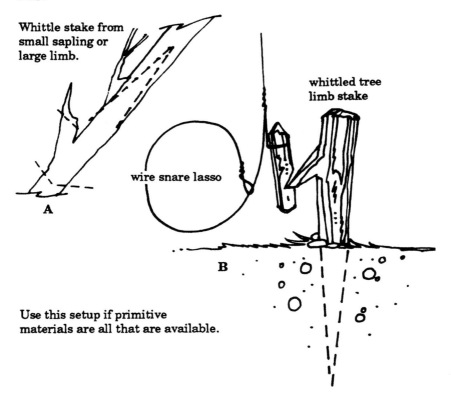

Whittle stake from small sapling or large limb.

whittled tree limb stake

wire snare lasso

A

B

Use this setup if primitive materials are all that are available.

Figure 21.

Got a nail, but don't feel like planting a stake to secure your trigger? Sometimes you can drive the nail into a log or tree stump instead of a stake. See Figure 22.

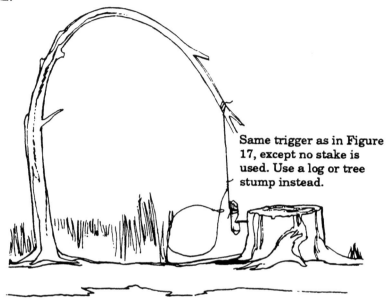

Same trigger as in Figure 17, except no stake is used. Use a log or tree stump instead.

Figure 22.

The trip-bar snare is used most often on an animal path, and sometimes at a den-hole entrance. It is normally not a baited snare, although it could be set up that way. It is essentially the same as the first simple snare except that the trigger is two poles that interlock within the pyramidal stakes. See Figure 23 for the details of this setup.

The next snare utilizes a somewhat different trigger and bait placement, and is a very effective snare. Normally, it is a baited snare. See Figure 24 for details.

Two more snare sets are shown in Figures 25 and 26. The front-and-back snare (Figure 25) uses two snare

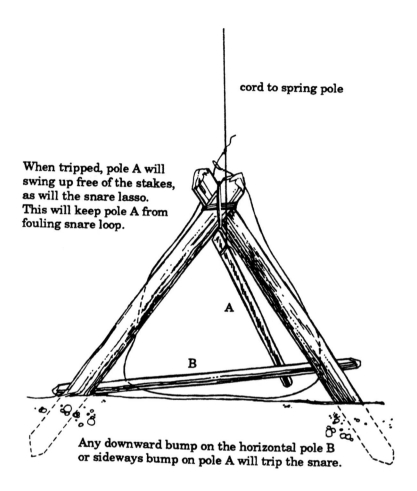

cord to spring pole

When tripped, pole A will
swing up free of the stakes,
as will the snare lasso.
This will keep pole A from
fouling snare loop.

A

B

Any downward bump on the horizontal pole B
or sideways bump on pole A will trip the snare.

Figure 23. Trip-Bar Snare.

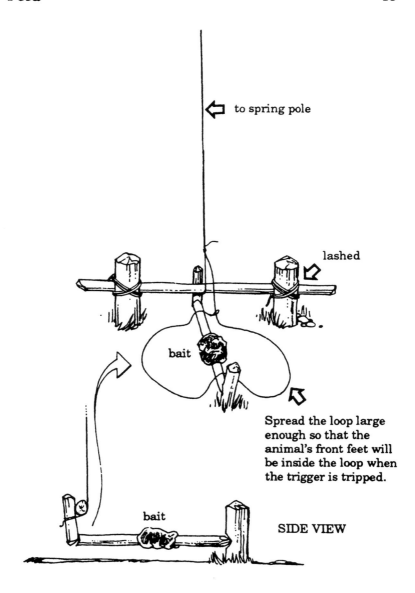

to spring pole

lashed

bait

Spread the loop large
enough so that the
animal's front feet will
be inside the loop when
the trigger is tripped.

bait

SIDE VIEW

Figure 24.

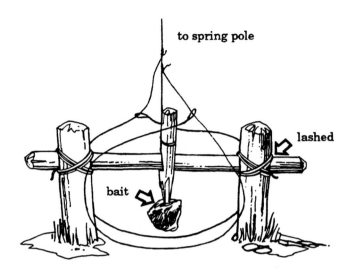

Figure 25.

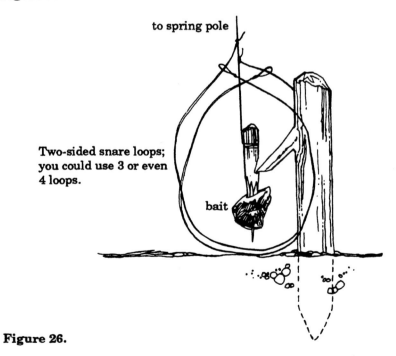

Figure 26.

lassos, one on each side of the bait. Figure 26 shows a variation of the trigger in Figure 21. Note that the whittled-peg trigger is longer and is also used for bait placement. By now, the general scope of snaring should be clear to you; the illustrations are self-explanatory.

The lift-pole snare is difficult to categorize. It does not use a spring pole, and is only vaguely similar to the weight-over-a-limb method. It can be used on either an animal path or den hole, or it can be baited in a box-canyon set with equally good results. The amount of weight used can be adjusted to the size of the desired prey. The best description may be to say that it is simply a good general-purpose snare. See Figure 27.

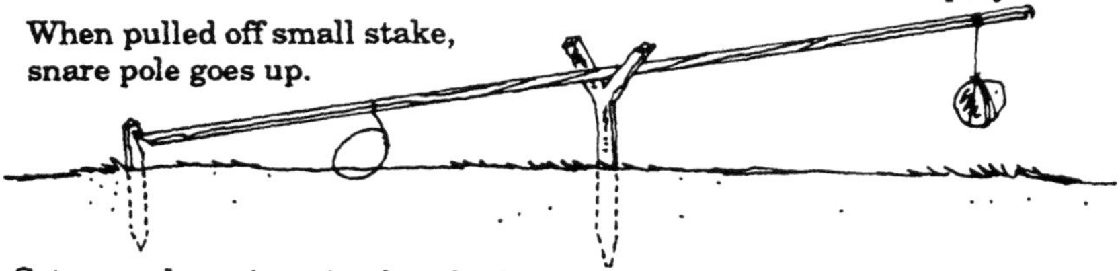

Amount of weight can be adjusted to the size of the desired prey.

When pulled off small stake, snare pole goes up.

Set snare lasso in animal path, den hole, box canyon, or other locations.
Figure 27. Lift-Pole Snare.

Small-Snare Refinements

There are several things you can do after you get the basic concept of snaring down pat. These little "tricks of the trade" will enhance your snaring success ratio.

The first is a trick with the wire lasso itself that will help it snap closed when jiggled only slightly. Figure 28 shows the small wire lasso that we made previously (we have already seen some variations in its use). There is a slight bump in the wire lasso just below the lasso loop.

Assume that the lasso is formed, not as you see it, but at the dotted-line juncture at point B. If it is formed thus and you pull the loop back so that it rests on the

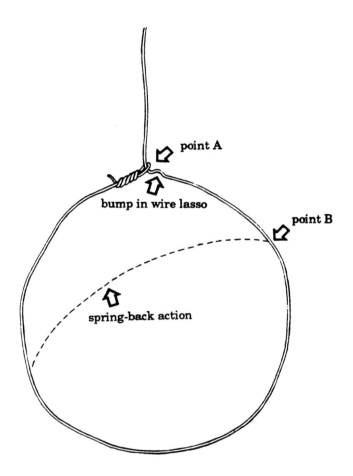

point A

bump in wire lasso

point B

spring-back action

Figure 28.

small bump in the wire you have formed at point A, the wire will be stiff enough so it will snap back to its dotted-line position with barely a touch.

What this does is help the snare close on the animal *before* the trigger is tripped and ensure that the trigger *will be* tripped. The wire from point A to point B should be as smooth and bump free as possible to facilitate this spring-back action. This little refinement takes some practice and is not easy to master, but it will increase your snaring production.

Another little trick to aid tripping the trigger is to make two connections on the whittled-peg trigger, one to the spring-pole cord, and one to the wire lasso itself. This provides a very fine trigger, easily tripped. See Figure 29.

Another refinement makes the trigger trip a little quicker than normal. Run a thread of similar small string from the trigger to the snare wire. The technique and purpose will be obvious as displayed in Figure 30.

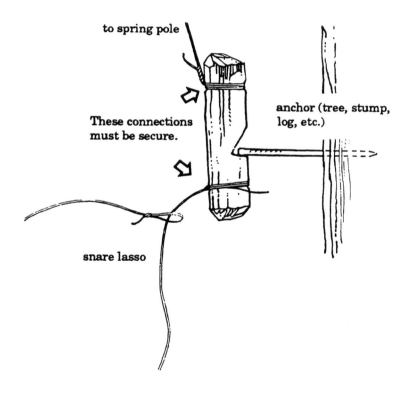

Figure 29. Trigger Variation.

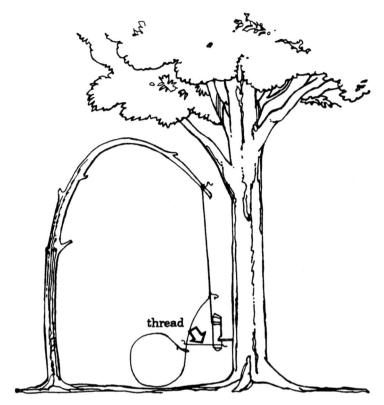

Figure 30. Thread-Trip Snare.

Still another variation, although not really a refine-ment, involves using a loop on the end of your spring-pole cord. The lasso is connected just above this loop. In this way, you can set the trigger without the whittled-peg release. The principle behind this setup is that a tug on the snare lasso will pull the spring-pole-cord loop off the peg. Note that the loop at the arrow must be set for a very fine, hair-trigger release, and the spring-pole pull strength must not be too great, or this setup will be difficult to trip. See Figure 31. The next release carries the same system one step farther. See Figure 32.

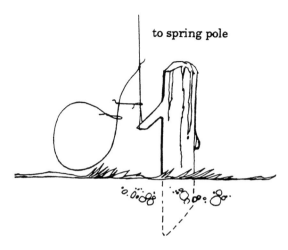

to spring pole

Figure 31.

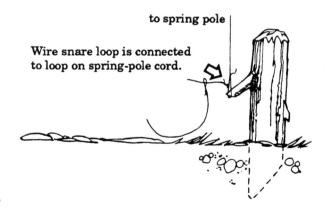

to spring pole

Wire snare loop is connected
to loop on spring-pole cord.

Figure 32.

Figure 33 shows a double snare that is excellent for box-canyon use. It greatly enhances the likelihood of your snare making a catch, simply because there are two lassos the prey will have to get past instead of one. It is especially useful when you know the animal will be approaching the bait from a certain direction.

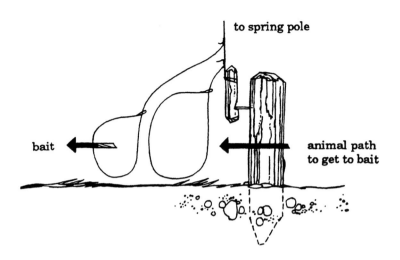

to spring pole

bait ←

animal path
to get to bait

Figure 33. Double Snare.

As stated before, the only thing I do not recommend varying is the wire lasso itself. Do not try to use rope or cord or anything that is not wire on these small snares. You can vary the thickness of the wire for different size game, but *use wire.* Later in this book, cable will be used for large game such as deer but, again, using any size rope or cord for the lasso itself usually does not work well.

Also, do not expect to get good results if you fail to use a spring pole or weight. The anchor-to-snare system, with no jerking motion, does not work as well as some authors and snare makers would have you believe. You may have some success with it, but you will have more success with a spring pole or weight release.

Do study the drawings shown. Variations are possible. Learn the details and techniques by doing! Adapt to the conditions. Use what is available. Be creative!

Large-Animal Snares

Of the people in this country who make use of the following snare, most would call it a "deer snare." I hesitate to do so, because it is good for a wide variety of large animals. The design will work on deer, elk, moose, and other game of such size.

The chief motivation for setting the large-animal snare is to secure a large amount of meat in one catch. The larger snares are not used as much for fur taking.

Snaring large game calls for a different approach than that used to snare small animals. Consider the wire lasso. Logic will tell you that when snaring a large animal like a deer or elk, a few strands of copper wire are not going to hold it. Also, no spring pole is going to jerk such a large animal off its feet and into the air. This would be counterproductive even if it were possible.

What you desire in a large-animal snare is one to hold the animal or at least drastically slow its movement away from the snare site. You want the snare to be made so that it will not loosen and allow the animal to get its head out, but you don't want it to tighten to the point that it strangles the animal. Meat spoils quickly outdoors—you want the animal to be alive and healthy when you get to it. This point is important to remember because this type of snare almost always catches the animal around the neck, while the smaller snares rarely do. Thus, for large animals, although the techniques are much the same as for smaller animals, you will need a slightly different type of snare.

In northeast Texas, where all of my tinkering with snares of this type has been done, there are no elk or moose, only white-tailed deer. So, the snare set which follows will be tailored for white-tailed deer. With minor changes for different game and game habits, you can adjust the snare for your particular locality.

The first thing you must do when using a whitetail snare is decide on a location. Normally, a whitetail snare is not a baited trap, and only extremely unusual conditions might allow you to draw deer into a snare. An example might be a home garden with a fence around it tall enough that the deer could not jump it. If the crop in the garden was something the deer craved, such as peas, you might be able to set a snare at the gate into the garden with some chance of success. But whitetail snares are normally set on heavily used deer trails.

You'll need to know the deer trails in your neck of the woods, and you'll need a sizable population of deer. *Note:* Do not set a whitetail snare in an area where you see deer only once in a great while. The reason for this is that you need to check this snare at least every day. In an area where there are few deer, you will run yourself to death checking it every day, unless it is close to your home, and it might be quite a while before you finally catch anything. Also, if the area is fairly well populated with deer, the trails they use are more apparent, and the chance of setting the snare in the right spot are greater.

The choice of a site is very important. Scout around for the paths you see the deer using most often. A deer trail is easy to spot once you really start to look for it. Find a site on the trail where there is some light brush or tall weeds on each side of a well-defined trail. These will be used to hold the snare up from the ground and in the desired shape and position. You want your snare to be *directly on* a well-traveled white-tailed deer route, and at some point on the trail where there is enough light brush or tall weeds on each side of the trail.

Now, with the location decided upon, you can proceed to make your snare. You will need the following items:

1   piece of one-sixteenth- to one-quarter-inch cable, approximately fifteen to twenty feet long
3   cable clamps (two will do in a pinch)
1   flat piece of metal with two holes
1   one-foot piece of kite string to use as a temporary line
1   piece of spring-pole cord of appropriate length
1   log or drag weight of about thirty pounds
    black electrical tape

Before we get into a detailed explanation, please study Figures 34 and 35. Armed with your general knowledge of snaring from the small snares and after studying the illustrations, the general scope of the whitetail snare should be apparent. Looking at Figure 34, we will go over the snare piece by piece.

The spring pole is triggered in exactly the same way as in the small snares. The same type of whittled-peg trigger is fine. The purpose of the spring pole itself is slightly different. On a whitetail snare, the spring pole's purpose is to merely snub the snare up tight around the neck when the deer walks through the snare, bumping off the trigger. The spring pole, of course, is not supposed to jerk the deer up in the air, as in a rabbit snare, or even to hold the deer at the snare site.

The snare itself is made from cable for strength. The diameter of the cable can be from one-sixteenth-inch to one-quarter-inch, but no smaller or larger than that. You will need a piece fifteen to twenty feet long in order to make the lasso and have enough line left for the slack coil and to attach to the drag weight.

The purpose of the short piece of temporary line is for it to break *after* the spring pole has been triggered and the lasso has been snubbed up on the deer's neck. It should not break instantly, but should be string of such strength that, when the deer begins to pull against it, it

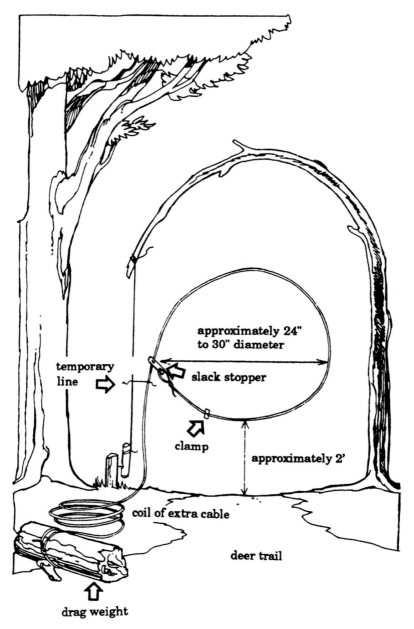

temporary line ⇨

approximately 24" to 30" diameter

slack stopper

⇦ clamp

approximately 2'

coil of extra cable

deer trail

⇧ drag weight

Figure 34. Large-Animal Snare.

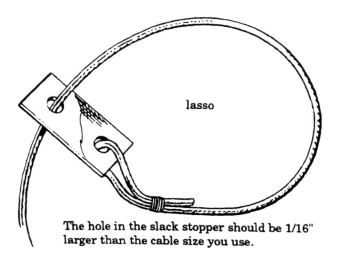

The hole in the slack stopper should be 1/16"
larger than the cable size you use.

Figure 35. Slack Stopper.

will eventually break. Kite string is about right. This
will leave the drag weight attached to the deer via the
cable lasso around its neck.

The purpose of the slack stopper is just as the name
implies. Once the snare is snubbed tight around the
animal's neck, this device will prevent the cable from
backing out as it would if it were merely passing
through a loop in the cable. The slack stopper can be
made from almost any type of metal. *Note:* You may
have to use black electrical tape to firmly attach this
temporary line to the cable just below the slack stopper.

The cable clamp on the line just down from the slack
stopper is to keep the lasso from tightening to less than
six or eight inches in diameter. This will keep the deer
from strangling itself as it pulls the drag weight. Put
this clamp twelve to fourteen inches down the line from
the slack stopper. *Note:* The three cable clamps are used
at the slack stopper, at the point twelve to fourteen
inches below the slack stopper, and to attach to the drag

weight. Depending on what you use for a drag weight and how you attach it, you might get by without this third clamp.

The drag weight is used for two reasons. A large animal like a white-tailed deer will fare better, and hence your meat for the freezer will be better, if it is not held fast in one spot once snared. The weight gives the deer a little freedom so it does not seem to get as upset as when it is held fast. I recommend about a thirty-pound weight. Even less weight can be used if the weight is difficult to drag because of its shape.

Second, the weight helps you find the animal because it will leave a trail behind the deer as it drags the weight around. The animal usually won't get far. A small log, as shown in Figure 34, will leave an easily followed trail.

As stated earlier, you will also need some small brush or weeds on each side of the trail to hold the lasso loop open and at the desired height. This brush or weed support is not shown in Figure 34.

This large animal snare is easy to make and is not expensive, even if you have to buy all the components. It can be made with very small cable for smaller game, such as foxes and coyotes. With the smaller snares, it will not always be necessary to use a drag weight. Foxes, coyotes, and the like can be held at the snare site by attaching the cable directly to the spring pole.

This snare, as with most of the traps in this book, has many possible variations for use in different parts of the country. Be creative. Good luck.

OTHER TRAPS

Let's leave snaring behind us and look at some other traps. Like the snares, these traps are open to variation. Each set could be made slightly different to accommodate the building materials available. The idea is to get the basic trap's construction firmly in mind so that, if you have to, you can improvise.

Hinged Box Trap

First, we will look at the hinged box trap. Basically, it is a box open on both ends. On the open ends, a door is hinged at an angle so it can be pushed in from the outside, but not pushed out from the inside.

The trap is more effective if the doors are some type of metal grille, so the animal can see completely through the box. However, this trap works reasonably well with solid doors. The box itself is generally solid wood, but could be made of some type of wire mesh (such as hardware cloth or poultry netting) around a framework of wood.

The hinges used on the doors do not have to be like the hinges on a door in your home. That type of hinge would be fine, but the doors could be lashed on with wire and still be effective.

The trap can be used with or without bait, and it works well in many locations. The size of the trap can vary considerably depending on the kind of animal you are trying to catch.

One end of the trap could be set flush at a den hole so that when the animal comes out of the hole, it will push its way past the first door and will be trapped in the box. From inside the den hole, the trap would merely look like the last two or three feet of the tunnel. The trap could be constructed with one end wired permanently shut if it's to be used solely as a den-hole trap. For an illustration, see Figure 36.

Armadillo Trap

The armadillo trap is very common in northeast Texas. The armadillo is a scaly little critter that likes to

The box can be solid wood or made from
wire mesh formed around a wooden frame.

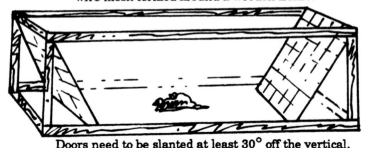

Doors need to be slanted at least 30° off the vertical.

Figure 36. Hinged Box Trap.

root up your yard, dig holes, and make a general mess of
your lawn. Generally speaking, it likes to do this between about 10 P.M. and 3 or 4 A.M. The armadillo trap is
commonly used in Texas without bait to catch these
destructive little devils.

First, using plywood, wood planks, or other suitable
material, build a box about 1 1/2 feet by 1 1/2 feet by
about 4 feet long, with both ends left open. The top
needs to be about one inch shorter on each end than the
sides and bottom.

Using molding of almost any kind, fashion a
slideway for the doors to fall through, and make a door
for each end. Build the upper support as shown in
Figure 37, and string the trigger. Cut a hole in the top
of the box for the trigger to rest against when set. If you
study Figure 37, the use and construction of the armadillo trap will be obvious. The principle of this trap is
that the weight of the doors allows them to drop when
the trigger is bumped off its catch in the hole on top of
the trap.

Why do armadillos go into this unbaited trap? I have
no earthly idea! My only theory (and it's just a wild
guess) is that, due to the armadillo's very poor eyesight,

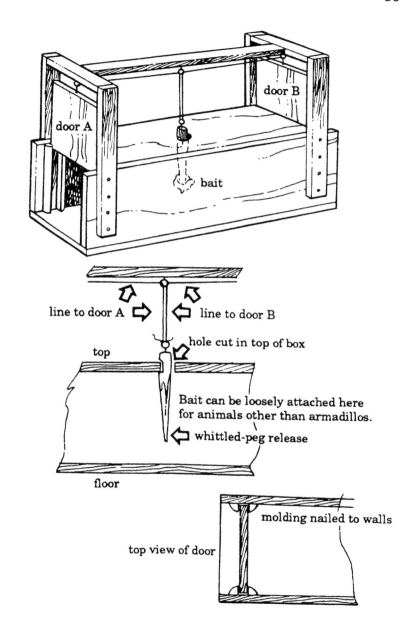

line to door A ⇨ ⇦ line to door B

hole cut in top of box

top

Bait can be loosely attached here
for animals other than armadillos.

⇦ whittled-peg release

floor

molding nailed to walls

top view of door

Figure 37. Armadillo Trap.

it may simply bump into the trap at some time during the night. Then, in an attempt to go around the obstacle, it goes down the side and into the open end of the trap.

I do know these traps work well. It is the only box trap I know of that works well without bait, but only for armadillos. Box traps usually use bait; this trap could be baited and used for other animals.

State of the Art

The box trap I refer to as the "state of the art" is simplicity itself, yet it can be triggered almost by a breath of air. The bait does not even have to be tugged. The pan that holds the bait can be merely touched, and the trap will spring. It can be made from around-the-house-type junk, as can most of the traps in this book.

At this point, please go back to Figure 37, our armadillo model. The state-of-the-art trap is identical except for the added bait pan and trigger inside the box. This difference makes the trap more difficult to build, but does make it extremely sensitive to being tripped.

First, construct a bait pan with a round wooden rod running through it. This round wooden rod is called a "full round" if you buy it at a lumberyard. Its diameter is not very important—an inch in diameter or less will be about right.

The full round is pushed through the holes in the bait pan and nailed firmly in place, so that when the pan is moved, the rod is twisted along with it. See Figure 38.

Now, construct the trigger assembly. It is simply a small wheel or spool around an axle of some sort, driven into the top of the full round. The example in Figure 39 shows a bent nail with some type of spool. This spool could be made of almost anything, as long as it will spin

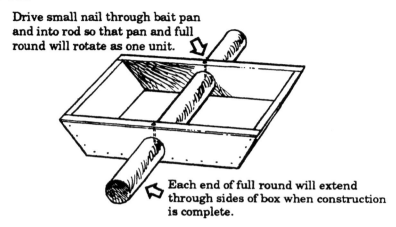

Drive small nail through bait pan and into rod so that pan and full round will rotate as one unit.

Each end of full round will extend through sides of box when construction is complete.

Figure 38. State-of-the-Art Trap.

fairly freely on the axle you use. *Hint:* broken appliances, especially cassette players and car stereos, have oodles of little spools inside them. Got a ruined audio cassette tape? Break it open and look inside. Even a short piece of dowel rod with a hole drilled through it lengthwise will do. See Figure 39.

Next, make the whittled-peg trigger. It needs to be a flat piece of wood (more plank than twig) wider than it is thick, and long enough to extend from the trigger assembly and out the top of the box. See Figure 40.

The reason for this peg being of such dimensions is that the hole cut in the top of the trap will be cut to minimize the chances of the whittled peg catching on the top of the trap. For example, if the peg is a half inch thick and one inch wide, make the slot in the top of the trap five-eighths inch or so. This slot can go all the way across the top. These dimensions will keep the peg from twisting and catching on the top of the box. Once tripped, the peg has nowhere to go but straight up, allowing the doors to fall.

Next, the bait pan (with trigger assembly connected)

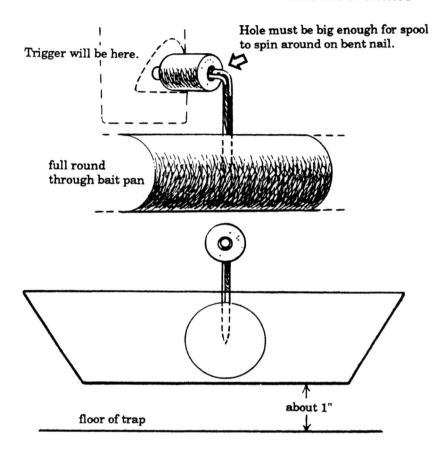

Trigger will be here.

Hole must be big enough for spool
to spin around on bent nail.

full round
through bait pan

about 1"

floor of trap

Figure 39.

is placed into the box so that when the bait pan is
touched, it will rotate the rod and pan one way or the
other. See Figure 41.

   This trap can be constructed with an extremely
delicate touch. Any upward or downward movement of
the bait pan will roll the spool off the trigger and spring
the trap. It is ideal for hard-to-catch creatures that will
not spring other traps.

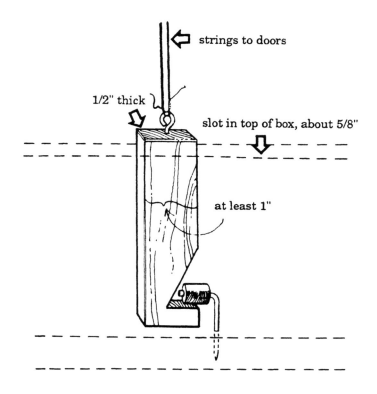

Figure 40.

Log Slam Armadillo Model

This trap is a variation of the basic armadillo trap. Instead of the doors sliding down a channel and shutting, they are hinged to close when the trigger is tripped. Log weights are placed atop the doors to slam them shut. The stakes are driven into the ground at an angle at strategic points at both ends of the trap. These stakes help lodge the log weights firmly against the door on the outside so that it cannot be pushed out from inside. See Figure 42.

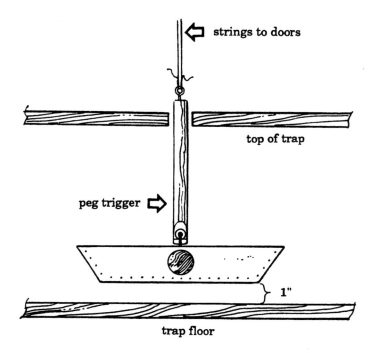

Figure 41.

Block Trap

Do you want to make a few small survival traps to take to the woods with you? The block trap is easy to make at home. It is generally made extremely small for squirrels, raccoons, and other small animals. I have seen large metal models made for bears, but generally speaking, these traps are made for smaller, grasping animals such as raccoons.

What I do not like about this trap is the pain it inflicts on the trapped animal until you can return to check the trap and kill the trapped animal. This trap should be used only as a survival measure.

The first thing you need is a block of wood. A piece

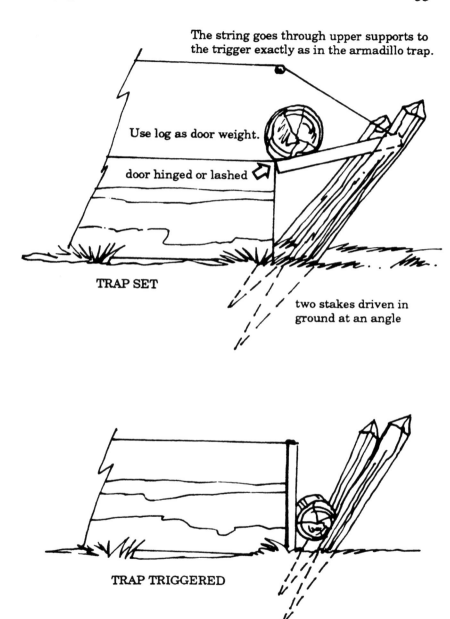

Figure 42. Log Slam Armadillo Trap.

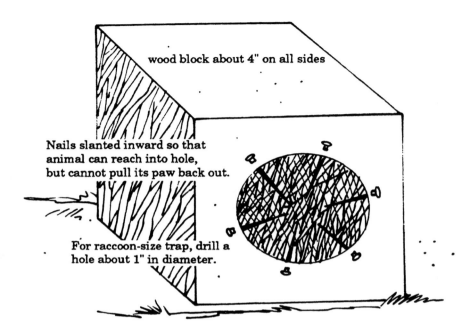

wood block about 4" on all sides

Nails slanted inward so that
animal can reach into hole,
but cannot pull its paw back out.

For raccoon-size trap, drill a
hole about 1" in diameter.

Figure 43. Block Trap.

about four inches on all sides is about right. Drill a hole
into it about three-quarters of the way through. For raccoon and such game, a hole of about one inch in diameter is good.

Then, you will need five or six nails. Preferably,
these nails will be sharpened to a very sharp point with
a file. Drive them through the wood as shown in Figure
43.

You should also attach a small chain or cable to the
block on one side to anchor the block to something
stationary. It could be anchored by simply nailing the
block solidly into a large plank or onto a stump. In this
way, you will not need the anchor chain. However, this
may make retrieval of the trap for later use more
difficult.

Turn the block so that the hole is up. Pour into the hole in the block whatever you have decided on for the bait. Honey works well for most critters. Salt bacon cut in small pieces and dropped in is also good. Sprinkle a little bit around the outside of the hole, but concentrate most of the bait in the hole, especially if it is gooey, like honey.

The way the trap works is that the critter pokes his paw into the hole to get the bait. Going in, the paw passes the sharpened nails easily since they are slanted away. Trying to pull the paw out is a different matter entirely. The nails grab at the animal's paw, and the harder the animal pulls, the more the nails penetrate. See Figure 43.

Net Capture

The next transplant trap we will look at is the net capture. You have seen it in the movies a thousand times. What they do not show you in the movies is how it works. It is really very simple.

What it amounts to is a simple snare just like we have already rigged, except that instead of the snare wire going to a snare loop from the spring-pole cord, there are four cords going to the four corners of a net. See Figures 44 and 45.

The net capture is one of the few snare-like devices in which using a falling weight to jerk the net upward works as well, if not better, than using a spring pole. Either will work fine with this setup, however.

The only thing that is drastically different in design is to make the trigger extra long (seven or eight inches) and the stake in the ground as short as possible. You might have to cut out one link in the net if it is made of a small mesh, to allow the trigger to pass through. The trigger set (Figure 45), slightly different from our original design, and the spacing of the net on the ground will keep the net from catching on the stake once tripped.

Obviously, the net trap is *not* like the solid box traps we have seen earlier. Given time, many animals will chew their way out of a net capture. Thus, this trap needs to be checked frequently.

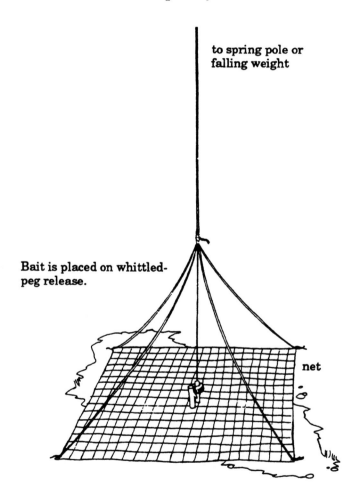

to spring pole or
falling weight

Bait is placed on whittled-
peg release.

net

Figure 44. Net Capture.

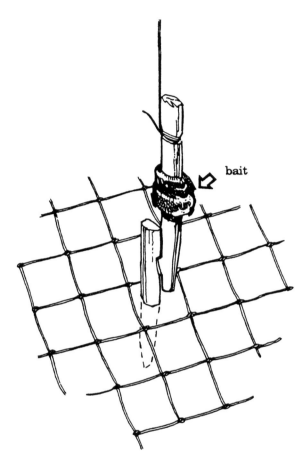

bait

Be sure to place net on ground so that when it is pulled upward, it will not catch on the notch of the stake in the ground. Cut one link in the net if necessary.

Figure 45. Detail of Net Capture.

CHAPTER TWO

Water and Fire

Food, as we have seen earlier, can be obtained in many ways. Water, on the other hand, is a little tougher to get. As with a lot of things in life, this works out exactly wrong. You can do with very little food for a long time if you have water. You may not be very comfortable, but you can survive for lengthy periods with little or no food. *But not water.*

Dehydration begins in two or three days, even if you do not exert yourself. It could happen even sooner, depending on the conditions. So, let's cover all we can about water gathering.

First, the obvious water sources are ponds, lakes, streams, and so on. In northeast Texas, a person would be very unlucky if he walked a half mile in any direction without running into a creek or pond. Water is everywhere. In other areas, however, water is not as plentiful.

WATER GATHERING

You can collect enough rain water to keep you alive

if you work at it a little bit and have some basic
materials. Putting out pots to collect rainwater generally won't get much. Even if it is a downpour and you
have twenty pots set out, you won't collect much by just
letting the rain fall into the pots.

Think about it. If you get a hard two-inch rain, you
will have approximately two inches of water in each pot,
depending on the shape of the vessel. Two inches in the
bottom of a pan is not much. If, however, you have even
a small tarp stretched out in such a manner that the
rain that falls on the tarp collects in one spot, you can
fill up a large barrel in short order in a hard rain.

The mathematics of this is easy, if simplified.
Suppose you had a small ten-foot square tarp set up in
this manner. All the rain water that landed on top of
the tarp would collect in one spot if you set up the tarp
correctly. What the tarp does is multiply the amount of
rainwater you can save by hundreds of times compared
to what you can collect in a bucket in the rain.

Plants are another source of water. In season,
berries are a good source of moisture. And, of course, so
is other fruit.

The prickly pear cactus is full of water. You can
scrape off the spines, chew the insides for the moisture,
and spit out the pulp.

With all plants, however, there is a problem: iden-
tification. Many plants in different areas of the world
are poisonous. There are many more that, while not
lethal, are somewhat toxic and will make you sick.

You simply cannot learn all the edible plants and
berries that exist and, more importantly, which ones to
avoid, from *any* book. Edible wild plants will have to be
learned from "hands-on" experience in the field *in your
area*. People who can teach you this are rare, but it is
knowledge worth having. Take a few field trips with
some old timers who are willing to pass on what they
know.

Another little tidbit that might help keep you alive is a little on the distasteful side. Lost in an area where there are simply no streams or ready sources of water? Really desperate? You won't be interested in this unless you are beginning to dehydrate, but insects provide moisture when eaten raw. The Australian aborigine makes use of insects in his desolate environment.

Solar Still

Are you not quite that desperate, but know you are going to be in an area with no stream water? Want to take something with you to prevent all this worry? Great. Take a sheet of plastic about six feet square. It should be the kind of plastic (poly) that you might find around your suit when it comes back from the cleaners, or the thin plastic that painters sometimes use for a drop cloth. With this plastic, and very little else, you can create the old standby, the solar still.

I started seeing this little setup about twenty years ago. I have no idea who invented it, but the technique is fairly well known.

First, try to select a spot for the water still that is as low in elevation as possible. The reason for this is that the lower the spot, the greater likelihood the soil will have some moisture in it. A creek bed is ideal. Even if dry, the bottom of the creek bed would probably retain some moisture in the soil a few inches down. Of course, you will have to use your own common sense. There are always exceptions to every general rule.

To start, dig a circular hole about three or four feet in diameter and about a foot and a half deep. Put a pan or cup in the bottom of the hole. Throw in some fresh-cut green plants around the cup, but do not cover the cup. See Figure 46.

Next, cover the hole with the piece of plastic. Pile dirt on the sides of the plastic to secure it over the hole.

Set stone to bring the plastic to a point directly over the cup or container.

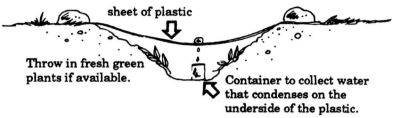

sheet of plastic

Throw in fresh green plants if available.

Container to collect water that condenses on the underside of the plastic.

Figure 46. Solar Still.

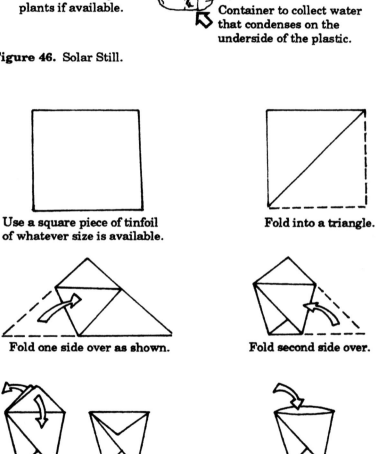

Use a square piece of tinfoil of whatever size is available.

Fold into a triangle.

Fold one side over as shown.

Fold second side over.

Fold one flap at top over front, and fold the other flap over the back.

Pop open cup with finger.

Figure 47. Makeshift cup.

Then, place a small stone in the center of the plastic so that it will be directly over the cup.

What happens is this: the freshly dug dirt will begin to give up its moisture into the air. The green plants you have thrown in will also contribute. The moisture will condense on the underside of the plastic, run down the plastic to the point provided by the stone, and drip into your container.

This still will provide enough water to keep you alive almost anywhere. It may not pull up the water by the buckets, but you can survive. Move the still every day, as the moisture in one spot will be given out by that time.

If no container is available, see Figure 47 for a homemade cup. If this cup is made of tinfoil or bendable metal, it won't leak. You can make the cup of paper for a quick drink, but the paper will become saturated after a few minutes and begin to leak.

WATER PURIFICATION

Even where water is plentiful, the battle is not completely won. Streams, ponds, and lakes rarely have good drinking water. They almost certainly contain some forms of bacteria and general trash particles, even if they appear to be clean. This may or may not be true of high mountain streams, but the penalty in ill health for being wrong is too great to take a chance. *Never* drink out of an unfamiliar water source unless you purify the water first.

Purification is a two-step process. First, you need to strain the water to remove particles of dirt and any small trash that is difficult to see. Then, with the water reasonably filtered, you need to boil it or purify it chemically.

You can use almost any type of cloth for a strainer. Even a shirt will suffice. Fold the cloth in several layers if the material is loosely woven. You want the straining material to be thick enough so that it takes a little time for the water to trickle through. I'm told a felt hat makes a good water strainer.

After straining the water into your container, the easiest way to kill the bacteria is to boil the water. You should boil it vigorously for at least five minutes. Unfortunately, the boiling gives the water a flat taste; this can be helped somewhat by pouring the water back and forth a few times from one container to another to aerate it. At any rate, a flat taste is a small price to pay to avoid getting sick from drinking water containing toxic bacteria.

Chemical purification is another option. Before a trip, purchase chlorine tablets to purify water at the drugstore. After adding the tablets to the water, let it stand for about half an hour.

Household bleach can also be used to purify water. Ten drops per gallon is the correct ratio. Use twelve drops if the water is extra grungy. Again, let the water stand for about half an hour after treating it before use.

Personally, I prefer boiling to any chemical treatment. There is something about putting bleach (even a few drops) into my drinking water that I cannot quite get accustomed to mentally.

FIRE

This section on fire is divided into three parts: tinder, match-type fire sources, and nonmatch fire sources. All three sections list ideas that will work and produce the desired result: a fire for warming, cooking, or signaling. As with almost everything in this book, the reader will have to use whatever is available at the time. This section deals strictly with getting a flame going. The exact setup of a cooking or warming fire will be dealt with later in the section on campcraft.

Tinder

The most difficult thing for most people to master in building a fire in the wild is the importance of taking their time in preparation. It is easy to get in a hurry when making a campfire in order to get on with other things. Sometimes this hurrying results in general frustration and a fire that is stubborn to light.

Tinder is whatever fuel you use—usually small sticks—that lights easily and will burn long enough to cause the larger pieces of wood in your fire to start burning. Let's begin with primitive tinder, and work our way up to a case in which some more modern materials might be available.

Scenario 1: You have a tarp stretched out for some protection from the elements. You also have matches, but no easy modern fire starter like gasoline. To make matters worse, it has been raining for a solid hour and the woods are soaking wet. This has effectively eliminated your chances of using dry leaves as tinder. It is also within a couple of hours of nightfall, and you feel you need to get a campfire going reasonably quickly. You need dry tinder to get a flame going and larger dry pieces to burn once the small flame is established.

In the woods, you can almost always find limbs that have broken off taller trees and have fallen and lodged into brush or smaller trees below. These small limbs will make good tinder even if they are wet on the outside. Don't bother picking up any wood that is lying directly on the ground it will generally be soaked through. Gather as many limbs lodged in the brush as possible and transport them back to your camp. Gather more than you think you will need to get the fire going. At the camp, put them under your tarp to dry further, while you go back to gather the larger wood.

At this point, let's consider other sources of small tinder in case you cannot find an abundance of brush-lodged limbs. If you have ever been in woods where there are pine trees, you have undoubtedly seen what the old timers call "heart-pine stumps." I do not know how scientific that description is, but what they are is this: stumps of pine trees long since dead and mostly gone. The only thing left sticking out of the ground is the stump that was once the "heart" of the pine tree. After years of weathering, the rest of the tree has rotted away, and the heart-pine stump is literally hard as a rock. However, it is still filled with pitch that somehow preserves the stump almost forever. It is a fantastic fire starter. Take your hatchet, knife, or whatever, and chop off all the tiny splits you can from these stumps. If you can pull up the entire stump, do so. This type of wood is the most potent natural fire-generating tinder I have ever seen.

What if there aren't many limbs lodged in brush off the ground, and no heart-pine stumps to cut up? Another little device to help get a fire going is to use fuzz sticks. If you can find *any* limbs at all, break some into pieces about six to eight inches long. These limbs need to be a little larger than kindling sticks generally are, somewhere between three-quarters-inch to one inch in diameter. Take each one and cut into it at an angle almost to the point of cutting off a small shaving, but leave the shaving attached. Fifteen or twenty of these sticks make good kindling. See Figure 48.

Figure 48. Fuzz Sticks.   Whittle shavings so they are almost cut off the stick, but leave attached.

A bird nest makes excellent tinder. These are quite often dry enough to burn, even after a rain. Most people would not think of using these nests, but collect all you can. Sometimes squirrel and mice nests can be used to advantage, too.

Now that you have tinder of one sort or another at your camp, collect larger wood. Use the same technique you used for the kindling, only look for the big stuff. You can almost always find some trees in the forest that are dead but still standing. The larger limbs of these dead trees can be chopped or broken off, and are usually dry enough to burn, even after a rain.

Sometimes a dead tree will fall, but its limbs will hold the main trunk off the ground. This tree will be dry on the inside, even after a rain. You may have to split it up into firewood, but it will usually burn.

After you have the limb kindling (or heart pine, or fuzz sticks) and the larger wood back at the camp, you are ready to start.

If your small tree-lodged limbs are still damp, take them and swish them in the air to remove any clinging moisture. If they are extraordinarily damp, you may have to split them lengthwise in order to get to the dry wood inside. For small twigs, this is usually unneccessary, but if needed, *do it*. Split these twigs into toothpick size if needed to provide dry wood for the best likelihood of the fire catching. This small kindling *must* catch and hold the flame in order to get the larger wood going.

After this drying and splitting process, sort these limbs into two sizes: a stack about two inches long, and a stack about six to eight inches long. Fifty to a hundred pieces of each size won't be too many.

Start by lighting the short two-inch pieces with your matches. These will catch fire easily enough. When you have a small stack of these going, gradually add the six-to eight-inch pieces, one or two at a time. Then, graduate to the smaller pieces of the larger wood. Soon, you should have a good campfire.

Scenario 2. This scenario is much easier than the rain-soaked woods. Suppose you are stranded in your car. It won't start, and you are in a secluded area where it appears you are going to have to spend the night. You have some matches. You're not worried about starving because you feel you can get help the next morning, but a campfire would keep away the cold.

No sweat. A car (even a wrecked one) or a downed aircraft provides lots of usable materials for firemaking. Look for an oil- or gas-soaked rag under the seat or in the trunk. Sometimes these will get a fire going.

No luck? Siphon some gas out of the tank. Even if you ran out of gas, there will usually be a little left in the bottom of the tank. No siphon hose? No problem. Open the hood and pull off the longest vacuum hose you can find from its connections and use it for a siphon. Once you have gas in the container, starting the fire will be easy. No vacuum hose long enough? Tie a rag on the end of a coat hanger, and run it down into the gas tank, thereby soaking the rag. You will still be able to get the gas with no siphon via this method.

Note: Don't puncture the gas tank to get gas out. You might create a spark that could cause the tank to explode. This would ruin your whole day, at the very least.

Perhaps your car, aircraft, or whatever, is totaled, and you are unconcerned about salvaging it. In that case, the cotton padding under the seats and the seat covers themselves will make reasonable tinder. There are many other flammable items in a vehicle, as well as fire sources, but right now we are concerned about tinder.

Look in the trunk. In some models, there is a heavy cardboard liner on the sides of the trunk. Peel this off in layers, and then tear up the layers into little pieces. Any paper source like this makes great tinder. Dump out the trash bag. Look for anything. Be creative!

Match-Type Fire Sources

Match-type fire sources provide a lesson in being prepared. The cost of outfitting your vehicles and equipment with fire-making sources is almost nil.

Consider the best little fire starter in the world, the cigarette lighter. Not the cotton-stuffed, flip-lid type in which the fuel dries out in a few days—we're talking about the cheapie little disposable lighter. Go to a discount store and you can buy a dozen of these lighters for about five dollars. Put a *couple* in each of your vehicles, especially in aircraft. Keep one (as well as a pocketknife) in your pocket as part of your usual routine. Do you have a tackle box, hunting pack, or camping backpack? Put a couple in each. These little lighters are useful for their convenience and longevity. I've had a couple in my fishing-tackle box for six or seven years now. They haven't dried out. They still light every time.

Not only that, these little lighters have an advantage over matches. They will put out a steady flame for as long as the fuel lasts to get a hard-to-start fire going. A match will burn out after a few seconds.

Matches can be stored away in much the same manner as lighters in tackle boxes, vehicles, and so on. For survival matches, it is best to do one of three things: (1) Make or buy containers for matches to keep them from getting wet, (2) paraffin the lighting end of the matches to waterproof them, or (3) both.

First, you should use large wooden kitchen matches. Book matches are almost worthless—better than nothing, but not by much.

There are waterproof match containers you can buy

in stores that sell camping gear. You can make your own with stuff from around your house. You can make a good container with two empty shotgun shells shoved together at the open ends with matches inside. It can be made better by taping the seam around the middle with tape.

Seal some matches in a freezer bag, then roll the bag into a cylinder and tape it. This will make it difficult for moisture to get to the match heads.

Another option is to protect match heads by dipping them in melted paraffin. The paraffin will dry, forming a waxy coating around the head of the match.

Your outdoor gear can be a storage place for reserve "desperation" matches. Often, a deep-woods hunter will take off the buttplate of his gun, drill a hole into the stock about half an inch in diameter, fill it with five or six paraffined matches, cork the hole with paraffin, and put the buttplate back on. Then (providing they don't lose the gun) they know they will always have some reserve matches if the situation gets desperate.

Other pieces of equipment, such as wooden frames for large backpacks, walking sticks, and so on, could be reservoirs for reserve matches also. These would have to be drilled in the same manner as the gun stock.

Another little trick to extend the life of a match flame is to use candles. Even tiny birthday candles will burn for four or five minutes, extending the life of your match's flame in a situation where your fire material is difficult to get going.

Coffee-Can Heater

Another little handy-dandy fire helper is a coffee-can heater. It is hard to categorize this thing. I use it mainly for deer hunting. When I am ten feet off the ground in a deer stand, this little homemade heater provides an amazing amount of heat with no detectable smoke or

Figure 49. Coffee-Can Heater.

smell. See Figure 49 for details on how it is made, and then we will discuss several ways it can assist us.

To make this heater, use a standard one-pound coffee can. Fit a roll of toilet paper into the can—it should be slightly smaller than the inside diameter of the can. Pour about one-fifth of a pint bottle of plain rubbing alcohol into the can, soaking the roll of paper. Save the rest of the bottle of alcohol for later fires. Once the toilet paper is soaked, light it with a match.

This heater is like a campfire I can carry with me. One bottle of rubbing alcohol will make about five separate fires, and each fire will last about fifteen minutes. You can use more or less alcohol, and thereby vary the length of time the fire will burn. If you use half a bottle or more of fuel, the fire will burn for about an hour without stop. I do not really understand why this little gizmo works so well, but I have used it for many years and it does work well.

Suppose, however, that you had the materials for this setup, but no matches. Any kind of spark you can generate will flame this little heater, which will then give you a steady flame for at least fifteen minutes. If a person cannot get his other tinder going in that length of time, he is in trouble anyway.

Another scenario where this device might help you is this: suppose you only had two or three matches and you were desperately wanting to conserve them. This little heater will fire with only one match, allowing you to get a conventional fire going without being worried about running out of matches. It will extend considerably the flame life of each match you have. The uses for this heater are many.

Non-Match Sources

Lenses. Lenses are probably the best and easiest non-match source for building a fire. Of course, the best magnifying glass in the world will not do you a lot of good at night, but this fire source is easy to use on a sunny day.

Get a good supply of fire tinder and wood ready as described earlier, and use the lens to focus the sun's rays at one small point on the tinder. Soon it will start smoking. Keep holding it on the spot until a flame appears and is well established on the tinder.

The most difficult thing about this method is holding the glass in one spot long enough to get the fire going. You will more than likely have to brace the hand you are holding the glass with against something—your leg or a log, for example—to keep it steady. This will enable you to be steady. The tinder will generally start smoking after a few seconds, but the appearance of the actual flame may take a few concentrated minutes of holding the magnifying glass *very* steady. The amount of time it will take will depend on a number of things, such as how good your tinder is, how cool or warm the weather is, and how sunny the day is.

The tinder you use in lens fire starting needs to be very small and dry. By small, I mean toothpick size or less. Dead pine-tree needles are good, but they must be brown and very dry, almost powdery.

A little refinement that can be used, if available, is a shiny piece of galvanized metal. Lay it in the sun for half an hour or so if it is a hot day, with your tinder lying on it. This will increase the starting temperature of the surface of the metal and tinder, and you will have to generate less heat with the lens to reach the flame point (at least by a few degrees).

Lenses can be stored in most of the places we discussed earlier for lighters. However, if you don't have a lens and your situation is desperate, one can sometimes be improvised. If you are stranded in a downed airplane or a disabled car, sometimes a piece of curved glass can be made to suffice. Check the lightbulbs under the dash and the headlights and taillights to see if their shape, broken into pieces, is appropriate. Sometimes a beam of sunlight can be focused with a broken piece of irregular glass.

Got a camera? There is always at least one lens in a camera, sometimes more depending on the model. Binoculars are a good source, as is the telescopic scope on a rifle. Admittedly, you would not want to break up expensive equipment unless you were really desperate, but the situation could arise.

Winter, and lots of ice available? I've been told a chunk of clear ice without bubbles can be shaped to make a lens. This sounds pretty desperate to me, and I have my doubts that it is even possible, but you might try it if all else fails.

Disabled cars and aircraft can provide some good nonmatch fire sources, also. Have you ever jumped a car with jumper cables? It almost always produces sparks when you first connect the cables. In this manner, you can produce sparks to get some tinder going. This is a modern version of the old flint-striking technique of creating sparks. The sparks won't do a great deal for stick kindling, but something more easily started, such as a gas-soaked rag, will start in a second. If you can scrounge a little gasoline to go on your wood kindling, the sparks will serve as an igniter. Obtain gas by using the method mentioned in the previous section on tinder.

Steel-Wool Fire. Perhaps the neatest little nonmatch fire source I've seen uses two fresh "D" size flashlight batteries along with some steel wool and fine dry kindling to get a flame going. I had heard about this method for a while before I saw it demonstrated. Before actually seeing it, and then doing it myself, I had never given it much thought. It sounded so unreal that I figured it was one of many such stories you hear (like moss only growing on the north side of trees) that are simply not true. But this one actually works.

This is how. Take two fresh flashlight batteries (the D size seems to work better than the smaller batteries) and hold them together end to end in your hands just as they would be arranged if they were in the flashlight. Take a piece of steel wool and hold it firmly against the bottom of the lower battery. Stretch the piece of steel wool up the side of both batteries and touch it to the top of the top battery.

The steel wool conducts electricity well enough to start to spark and actually burn. There is, however, nowhere near enough electrical current for you to feel it. Blow on the steel wool, encouraging the sparking, burning action, and use this to get your tinder going. It's amazing to watch.

You could probably do the same thing by using wires connected to a car battery and then to the steel wool (perhaps even something other than steel wool). But you probably wouldn't want to be holding the steel wool in your hands in that scenario. Be careful with variations of this technique!

These methods of generating an electrical spark would be good igniters for the coffee-can heater we discussed earlier, if you had no matches.

Bow-and-Arrow Fire Starter. The bow-and-arrow fire starter such as the Native Americans used is high on the order of difficulty. Even with all the proper materials and a good technique, it is not easy.

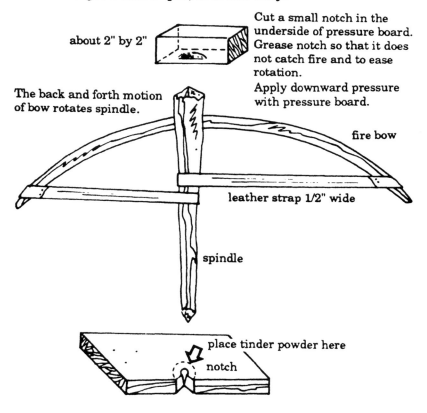

about 2" by 2"

Cut a small notch in the underside of pressure board. Grease notch so that it does not catch fire and to ease rotation.

The back and forth motion of bow rotates spindle.

Apply downward pressure with pressure board.

fire bow

leather strap 1/2" wide

spindle

place tinder powder here

notch

Figure 50. Bow-and-Arrow Fire Starter.

Several things are required. First, you will need a piece of leather half an inch wide, or some such material for the bow string. The bow itself needs to be about thirty inches long, with a diameter of a half inch or so. It does not need to be very springy.

You'll need a spindle about half an inch in diameter and about twelve to sixteen inches long to rotate. Sharpen it bluntly on one end and round off the other end. There is a difference of opinion as to whether an octagon-shaped spindle or a round one is best. Both will work. Most people prefer the octagon-shaped spindle for less slippage.

You will also need a small, flat piece of wood with a small notch cut in the center (for the rounded end of the spindle to fit into) to apply pressure on the spindle. And, last but not least, you will need a flat board with a notch cut into the edge for the sharpened end of the spindle to fit into. The spindle and the flat board with the notch on the edge need to be made of old, dry wood.

You will, of course, need some dry tinder ground into almost a powder to go in and around the spindle; this will ignite when the friction created by the rotating spindle reaches the flame point. See Figure 50 for details on this ancient fire-making setup. The bow-and-arrow fire starter is difficult to use at best. Be patient! It may take a number of tries to master the technique.

CHAPTER THREE

Shelter

If you are going backpacking through a remote wilderness and have the opportunity to prepare in advance, the modern tent is perhaps the best way to go. Personally, I prefer a forty-foot motor home, but in primitive situations such as we are dealing with throughout this book, modern tents are hard to beat.

Such a tent has many advantages and very little in the way of drawbacks. Chosen wisely, you can have a tent that is roomy, with its own floor, a zip-up entrance and screened windows. It will have its own tent poles. It also usually has its own carrying case, folds up to very small size, and is lightweight and generally inexpensive. I have a small dome tent that cost less than thirty dollars, sleeps two comfortably (four if necessary), and is easy to set up.

The only drawback to most modern tents is that they are not heavy duty enough to use for extended periods of time. They are usually made of nylon, which is less durable and will not last nearly as long as the old canvas tents. In addition, the seams do not seem to hold together as well over a period of use as the old-style canvas ones do. However, the fact that they are many times lighter than canvas and fold up to much smaller, more portable sizes is a definite compensating factor.

Given a situation where no advance preparation was done, such as one involving a downed aircraft or stranded automobile, you might be able to use part of the vehicle as shelter.

Barring that, a tarp can be made to suffice for shelter if a tarp is available. No tarp? How about a parachute? Heavy plastic sheeting? Even regular clothes sewn together will shed some water. Use whatever your brain and eyes can find for you. If you do have some sort of tarp, there are several ways you can use it.

TARP SHELTERS

Shelter can be easy if you are traveling and simply want to wait out a downpour in the dry and then move onward. If it is not a violent high-wind storm, but simply raining, take the tarp out of your backpack and spread it over you and your equipment and wait it out.

Perhaps the next best shelter is the tarp lean-to. There are a lot of variations possible, but the general design is as follows:

Cut a pole and lash it between two trees horizontally. This will be the front of your lean-to. Lash one edge of your tarp to the pole, using the grommets around the edges of the tarp. If your tarp has no eyelets (grommets), you will have to "bunch up" the material at the edge and tie the tarp to the pole via the knot you have formed with this material. Stretch out the other side of the tarp and stake it to the ground, forming an angle of 45 degrees or so. *Make sure* the contour of the ground will drain water *away* from your lean-to, not into it.

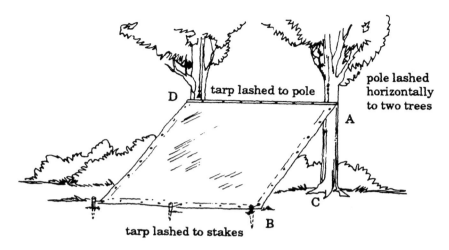

Figure 51. Lean-To Shelter.

Refinements

Once you have reached this point, there are a lot of refinements that will make this marginal watershed more livable. Let's consider some of them. In discussing these variables, it helps to look at Figure 51 for clarification.

1. Supports. There is a number of things that can be done to make the basic lean-to more stable. As it stands, it is little more than a sunscreen, and will shed only a light rain. Water from a heavy rain would tend to form a pool near the base in the center, and eventually the tarp would tear from the weight of the accumulated water.

To make it more sturdy, lash poles from the tree to the corners (points A to B on Figure 51), and correspondingly on the opposite side and at the center stake. The lower ends of these poles should be dug or driven into the ground at least a few inches. This will give the tarp firmer support, will keep it stretched a little more tightly, and will keep water from filling up on top as quickly.

2. *Lath.* If the shelter is to be used for several days or more, run smaller poles from the A-to-B poles to the corresponding pole on the opposite side, parallel to the A-to-D pole. These poles will need to be lashed *under* the A-to-B poles, or they will create the pooling action we talked about earlier. These lath poles are strictly for adding stability and strength to the framework.

3. *Sides.* By looking at Figure 51, it is easy to see that the tent would be drafty in a cold wind, due to the fact that the sides are open. They can be closed, however, in a couple of ways. If your tarp is large enough, it can be folded over the A-to-B poles and down to the ground. Lay a small log across the tarp to hold it down. Excess tarp can be rolled around the log and the log can be held in place by stakes as in Figure 52, if necessary. The log needs to be *inside* the lean-to, as in the illustration, to prevent pooling of rain water. If your tarp is barely large enough for the top of the shelter, you can improvise the sides. Drive in the ground from points B to C (in Figure 51) a series of vertical stakes that are lashed at their upper end to the A-to-B pole. Then you can weave in *tightly* some green limbs with leaves for a wind block and for some protection from a blowing rain. Do this for both sides. See Figure 53.

4. *Front.* If you have enough cord and the tarp is large enough, let the tarp extend over the horizontal pole (A-to-D pole in Figure 51) about a foot or two. It can be tied down in such a manner as to provide a watershed in the front, which will greatly increase your "out of the rain" space. See Figure 54.

5. *Inside.* On the inside, build a dirt wall six or eight inches high around the interior walls for keeping out water, much like a small earthen dam. This is a little added protection, since you have already set up the tarp in a location where the contour of the ground allows

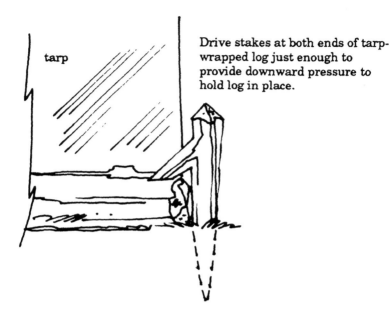

Drive stakes at both ends of tarp-wrapped log just enough to provide downward pressure to hold log in place.

tarp

FRONT VIEW

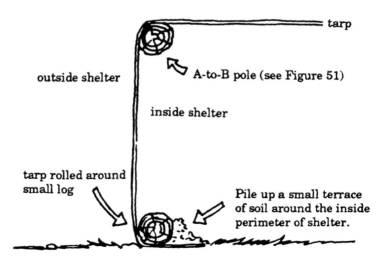

tarp

outside shelter

A-to-B pole (see Figure 51)

inside shelter

tarp rolled around small log

Pile up a small terrace of soil around the inside perimeter of shelter.

Figure 52.

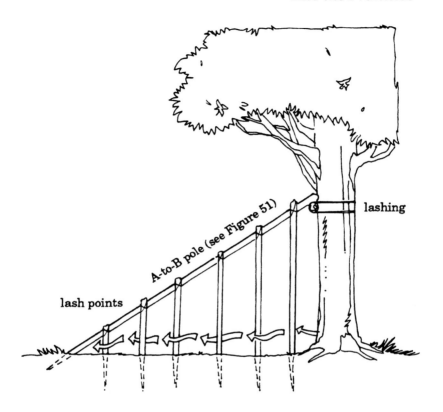

Figure 53.

water to drain away from, not under and into, your shelter. Remember, in considering a site for any shelter of this type, drainage in case of a downpour is an important factor.

6. *Alternate framework.* No trees available? The framework can be set up without the two large trees in Figure 51 if you can find some smaller saplings. See Figure 55.

Another easy shelter is the open-ended tent. The setup consists of tying a rope between two trees and

Extra tarp material extends over the horizontal
pole a foot or two and is staked with cord at a
downward angle to provide an "awning" off
the front of the shelter.

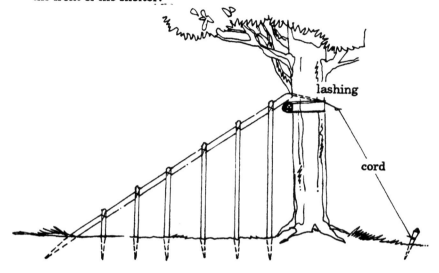

lashing

cord

Figure 54.

simply hanging your tarp over the rope and staking the
edges of the tarp down via the grommets. If you have no
long rope, a sapling could be lashed horizontally between two trees to support the tarp. A refinement would
be to close up one end of the shelter so that the wind
won't whistle through it. You can do this by tying the
grommets together on one end, allowing the floor area
to come to a point at the back of the shelter and be open
at the front. See Figure 56.

Figure 57 shows the same set as in Figure 56, but
with an alternate framework. Use rope to tie the stakes
directly in front of and in back of the shelter. This will
prevent the framework from collapsing in either direction.

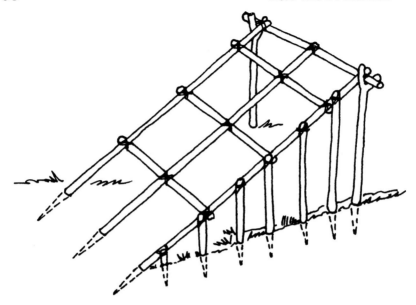

Figure 55. Alternate Framework.

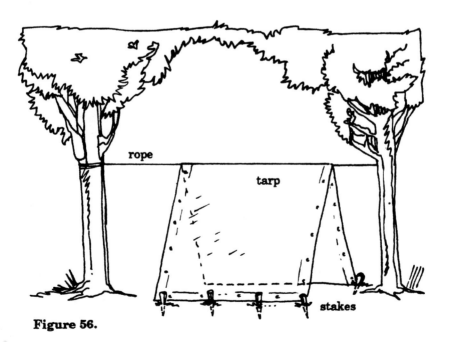

Figure 56.

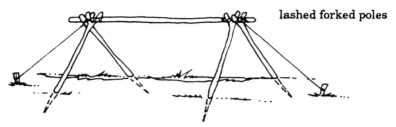

lashed forked poles

Using rope, stake directly in front of and directly in back of shelter. This will keep the framework from collapsing in either direction.

Figure 57. Alternate Framework.

Figure 58 shows another tarp-shelter framework that provides a lantern holder in front of the shelter. Cover the frame with the tarp, and secure the edges as in the previous examples. Is it already raining? Are you in a hurry? If a tree is handy, the long ridge pole may be lashed to it at a convenient height, thus eliminating the two forked support poles.

Tepee (or tipi) setups are more difficult and require a lot of work. In addition, they are difficult to move from day to day because the lodge poles have to be transported—they can't be cut anew for every camp without a monumental amount of work. To make matters worse, the covering has to be a custom fit, since a square tarp is not going to fit a cone-type framework.

However, something about the nature of tepees draws a lot of interest. I confess to being enthralled by

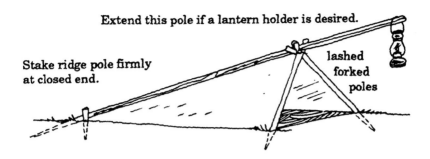

Extend this pole if a lantern holder is desired.

Stake ridge pole firmly
at closed end.

lashed
forked
poles

Figure 58.

them. For a semi-permanent camp, they are ideal. They
are large if you build them as the native Americans did.
Their ridge poles were around thirty feet long and
provided an eighteen-foot-wide (or so) oval floor. Also,
the original models usually had a smoke flap, rather
than letting smoke escape at the top juncture of the
ridge poles, as most modern tepees do.

Of course, you can build them whatever size and
style that suits you. They are cozy in cold weather since
a small fire can be built safely inside, provided you
leave enough ventilation for fresh air to enter. They are
the only tent-like structure I know of that you can have
a fire inside with reasonable safety. When building a
small fire inside the tepee, be sure to allow for some air
intake by leaving some ventilation. *Never* completely
seal off a tent from outside air. The fire will burn up all
the oxygen inside the tent. See Figure 59.

Stakes will almost always be required for pitching
tents or tarps around a camp. If you have advance preparation time, a good general-purpose stake can be made
with a piece of heavy flat metal. Drill some holes in it of
a size for which you have a peg. This stake can be
driven in deep or shallow ground via the peg placement.
See Figure 60. Two soft-ground wooden stakes and the
correct bevel for them are shown in Figure 61.

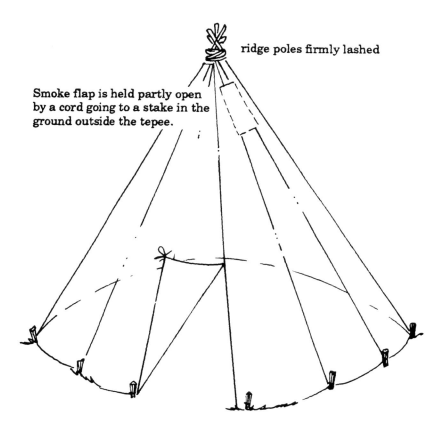

ridge poles firmly lashed

Smoke flap is held partly open by a cord going to a stake in the ground outside the tepee.

Figure 59.

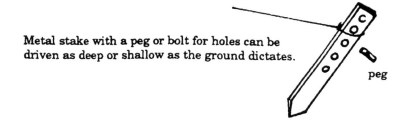

Metal stake with a peg or bolt for holes can be driven as deep or shallow as the ground dictates.

peg

Figure 60.

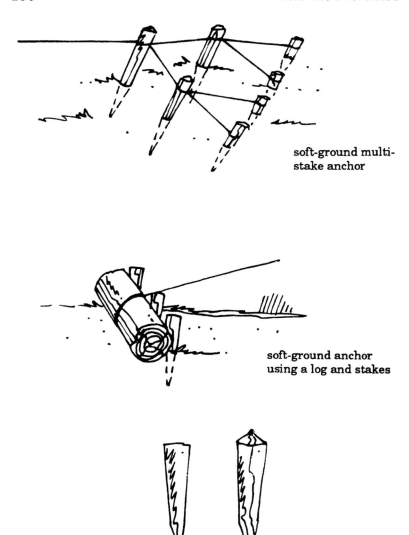

soft-ground multi-
stake anchor

soft-ground anchor
using a log and stakes

Bevel wooden stakes on the driving end to prevent splitting.
A flat-top sawed-off stake will split easier when being driven.

Figure 61. Stakes.

CHAPTER FOUR

Around the Camp

There are so many around-the-camp ideas floating around out there, one could write a long book on that subject alone. Campfire implements and many around-the-camp items can be made on the spot when needed.

COOKING FIRES AND UTENSILS

You have piled a circle of stones around in true boy-scout fashion and have a small campfire going in the center of the stones. You have let this campfire burn down to coals to provide an even cooking heat. You also have a pot to stew over the coals, but no grill on which to set or hang the pot. See Figures 62, 63, and 64 for several different schemes for cooking in your pot.

No cooking pot? Do you need to cook a big venison steak? Make a green-limb grill or spit, as shown in Figure 65.

Figure 66 shows a wonderful fire shelter and pot hanger, the structure of which can also be used for a bridge over a creek. The weight of the poles themselves

Adjust height of pot over fire   cooking fire (burn down to coals)
by moving support
back and forth.

Figure 62. Pot Hangers.

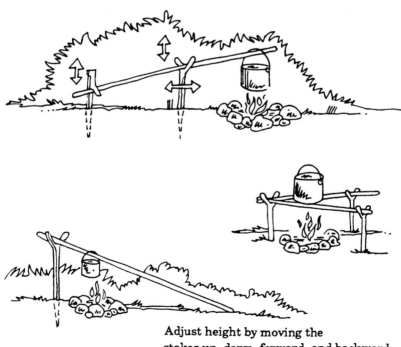

Adjust height by moving the
stakes up, down, forward, and backward.

Figure 63.

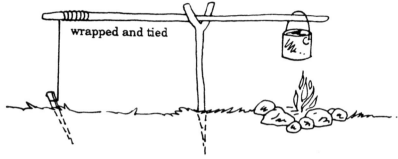

Adjust the height by wrapping or unwrapping
cord around the support pole.

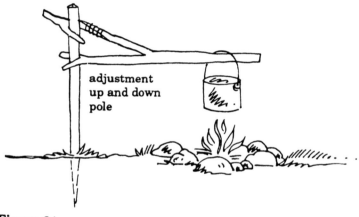

Figure 64.

will hold this setup together if they are interlocked as shown. If the poles are overly slick or barkless, some lashing may be needed. The added weight of the cooking pot actually adds to the stability of the frame. *No support poles can be used underneath.* If the frame is tall enough, you can lash a tarp cover on top to protect the fire from rain. You could even drape the tarp over the back of the frame if the tarp is large enough.

Other useful camp implements are shown in Figure 67. If you can salvage a flat piece of bendable metal, you

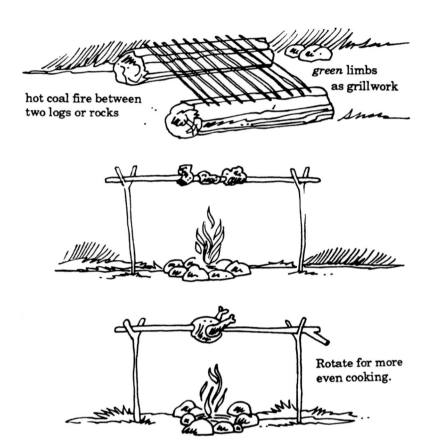

hot coal fire between
two logs or rocks

green limbs
as grillwork

Rotate for more
even cooking.

Figure 65.

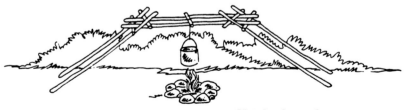

Height depends on
length of side poles.

Figure 66.

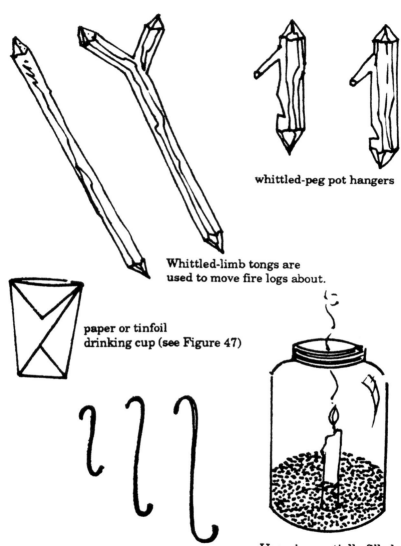

whittled-peg pot hangers

Whittled-limb tongs are
used to move fire logs about.

paper or tinfoil
drinking cup (see Figure 47)

Bent-wire pot hangers; use to adjust
height of cooking pot above fire.

Use a jar partially filled
with sand as a candle
holder and wind break.

Figure 67. Camp Odds and Ends.

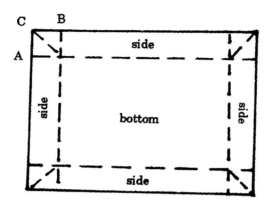

Figure 68. Cooking Pan.

can make a cooking pan as shown in Figure 68. To make
the pan, bend the corner of the metal so that point A
and B meet, with point C on the *outside* of the pan.
Bend the other corners in the same manner. Fold the
four "ears" (like point C) along the outside of the pan so
that the walls of the pan are vertical and as flat as
possible.

FURNITURE

Furniture is generally not worth the trouble it takes
to make *unless* (1) an extended camp of several days or
weeks is anticipated, (2) you are stranded in a remote
area and rescue may be a long time coming, or (3) you
enjoy the construction or the challenge of making these
items on site. In those instances, they can make life
more comfortable, especially the beds and chairs.

Tables, beds, and chairs are the pieces of camp
furniture that are easiest to make. Seats can be added
to the table in a picnic-table style if desired. Also, a
couple of varieties of camp-made hammocks are shown
in Figures 72 and 73. One will require a camp loom to

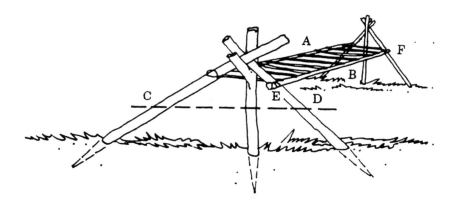

Figure 69. Basic Frame.

produce (also shown); the other is woven.

Figure 69 illustrates the construction of a basic frame structure that can be used to make tables, benches, and beds. To make the frame, sink a forked post in the ground. Insert straight poles in the ground at an angle and lash them to the forked post. Do this for each end of the frame. Lash two straight poles (E to F) to the angled supports to form the top surface of the basic frame.

Use whatever is available for the top itself. A series of small straight sticks lashed to the horizontal poles will suffice if nothing else is available. Seats can be added by notching and lashing poles as indicated by the dotted line from C to D. Horizontal poles for seats can then be lashed to these C-to-D poles and the angled support poles in the same manner as the horizontal poles used for the tabletop.

A simple chair is shown in Figure 70. Make two frames using one forked post and two straight poles, as shown. Sink the two base poles into the ground first, then add the seat-support pole. Use whatever is available to make the actual seat and back, such as small

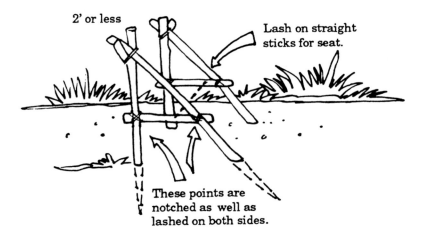

2' or less

Lash on straight
sticks for seat.

These points are
notched as well as
lashed on both sides.

Figure 70.

straight sticks. Support poles, at an angle from the side
of the chair to the ground, are sometimes needed for
stability.

You can make a bed using the basic frame shown in
Figure 69; use the two tabletop poles (E to F) for the
framework. If burlap bags (or some such material) are
available, cut the ends out of the sacks and push the
two poles through. These sacks can form a primitive
hammock, or can be stuffed with straw or other padding
material to make a mattress. See Figure 71a. If materials are available, sew a blanket around the poles to
support a person's weight. In a pinch, even heavy paper
bags (such as cattle-feed sacks) can be used. Another
option is to lay small sticks across the poles, as shown
in Figure 71b. Cover the sticks with pine needles or
similar material for padding.

If a good supply of string or cord is available, you
can weave a reasonably good hammock by using a loom
as shown in Figure 72. To build the loom, drive two
stakes into the ground and lash a crossbar as in the end
of the diagram. Tie cords from the bar at A to the stakes

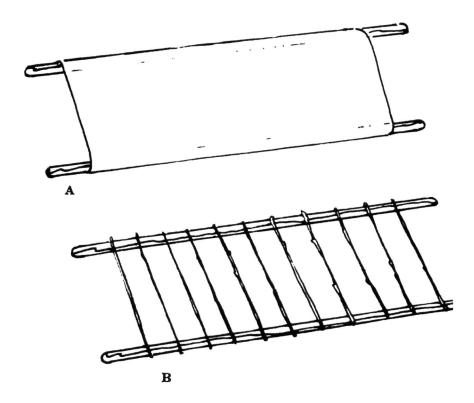

A

B

Figure 71. Beds.

at B. Then, tie cords from the C bar to the A bar, to alternate with the cords tied from A to the B stakes. By moving the C bar up and down, you can weave small sticks or tough grass into the hammock as shown at point D. When completed, the B end will have to be tied off to hold the weaving together. The hammock can be hung from ropes tied to the A and C bars.

Another hammock-weaving technique is shown in Figure 73. You will need two stout poles about three feet long. Stake them down about seven feet apart. Tie two lengths of cord to the poles from point A to F, B to G, and so on. String these cords tautly on the poles. Now,

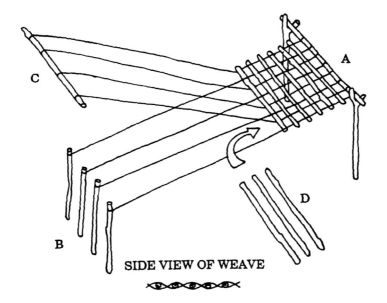

SIDE VIEW OF WEAVE

Figure 72. Hammock Loom.

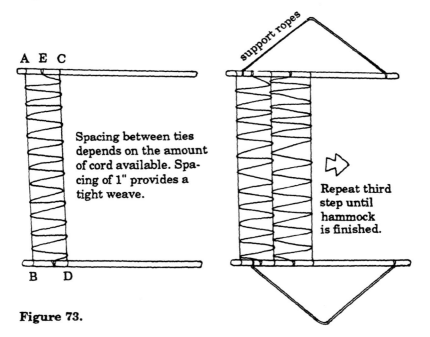

Spacing between ties
depends on the amount
of cord available. Spa-
cing of 1" provides a
tight weave.

Repeat third
step until
hammock
is finished.

support ropes

Figure 73.

tie a length of cord to the pole at point C, and weave the cord up and down over the A-to-F and B-to-G cords. Tie this cord to the opposite pole between F and G. Next, tie a cord parallel to the B-to-G cord and repeat the weaving sequence. Repeat these steps until the hammock frame is filled. When finished, the weave will resemble that of a chain-link fence. Tie support ropes to the poles on each end to hang the hammock.

KNOTS

There are quite a few different kinds of knots that can be learned for different uses. Once learned, however, most of them will never be used. A few basic knots will suffice for use around your camp.

The simple knot or thumb knot is used to put a stop on the end of a rope. This may be used to prevent the end of the rope from fraying, or as a lasso loop stop. See Figure 74.

Figure 74.

Next, a simple loop. It uses are almost endless. A simple or thumb knot is tied in the end of the rope and then a loop is formed as shown. See Figure 75.

Figure 75.

A lasso (Figure 76) is formed by making a simple loop, and then running the other end of the rope through the loop.

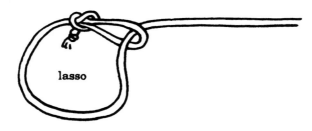

lasso

Figure 76.

At times, your rope may be too long for the job you are doing, but you want to avoid cutting it. A sheep-shank will shorten a rope conveniently. See Figure 77.

Figure 77.

An eyelet knot, shown in Figure 78, sometimes comes in handy. It is actually a simple loop with the stop knot around the main line.

Figure 78.

Figure 79 shows a knot useful for putting a series of loops in a line for things such as trotlines or harness loops.

Figure 79.

TOYS

At an extended camp, children tend to get restless with nothing to do. Nowadays, they get bored with lots of things to do, but that's another story. There are lots of little amusements that can be made in a matter of minutes that will keep the kiddos at least occasionally entertained.

A pair of stilts is always an easily made toy. There are two kinds to make; see Figures 80 and 81.

Trim two saplings as
shown to form stilts.

Figure 80. Sapling Stilts.

Grass whistles are amusing, and any time you can
scrounge up a blade of grass four or five inches long, you
can have a grass whistle. The grass is the reed, and
your hands make up the rest of the whistle. It sounds
more like the mating call of a pterodactyl than a
whistle, but it is a lot of fun for kids. By varying the
width of the grass reed you use, or the tightness of your
grip on the reed, a great deal of tone variation is possible (see Figure 82). This whistle makes a great crow call
with very little practice. *Note:* if the whistle isn't *loud,*
you haven't quite mastered it yet.

Punch two holes in opposite sides of a tin can.
Run a string through can, making a handle
for the stilts. Make two stilts.

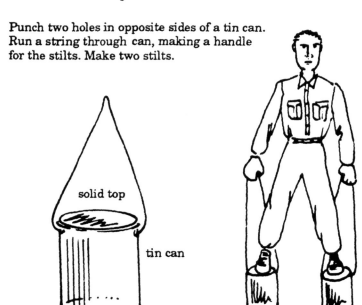

solid top

tin can

open end

Figure 81.

Darts are easy to make, and can be used in a game
of competition (see Figure 83). The darts are made by
rolling paper into a cone, taping or gluing the cone so it
will not unravel, and inserting a nail or some such
material as a point. The point can be made from whatever material can be scrounged, such as a pin with the
head cut off, a finish nail, a panel nail, or stiff wire. If
you use a small diameter point (a pin, for example), you
can tap it into the wood shaft with the point out. A pin
makes a good point for match-size to pencil-size darts. If
you use a larger point, you may have to split the end of
the shaft, insert the point, and then tape or bind it in
place. Make fins from paper—almost any type of paper
will do, as long as it is reasonably stiff. Make the split

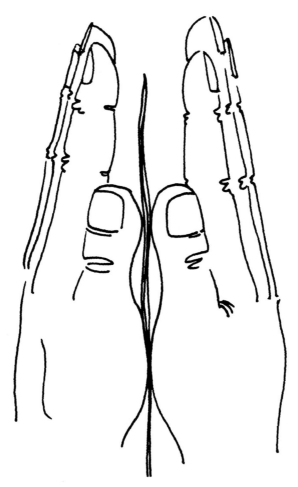

Figure 82. Grass Whistle.

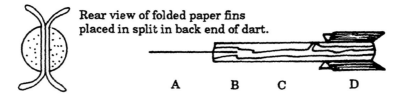

Rear view of folded paper fins
placed in split in back end of dart.

A   B   C   D

Figure 83. Darts.

in the end of the shaft only as long as the fin length, and they will hold tight without any glue.

A sling is a good camp amusement. Some primitive people hunt with these slings as weapons, but it seems difficult to believe that the degree of accuracy necessary for hunting could ever be achieved with a sling. However, I cannot personally hit anything with a boomerang either, and the aborigines have hunted with them for untold ages.

A sling is made by attaching two lengths of string to a pouch in the center. A throwing stone is folded into the pouch, which is usually made of leather. One string has a loop in it that fits around the index finger. The other string is held while the sling is whirled above the head so that it builds up centrifugal force. When the string being held is let go, the stone sails out of the pouch at great speed. Sailing a rock a hundred yards or so is no problem. See Figure 84.

Blowguns are a lot of fun. Of course, these should only be made for older, more responsible children. As with darts, blowguns can be dangerous, depending on the children involved. The power generated by blowguns is unbelievable to one not accustomed to using them.

To make a blowgun, you will need some modern tubing with a uniform inside diameter. Hollowed-out bamboo can be used, but the inside diameter of bamboo is not as consistent and cuts down the amount of force that can be generated. Use what is available. A tube about three feet long with a half-inch to five-eighths-inch inside diameter is ideal, but the length of the tube or its size is not very important when the blowgun is to be used as a toy. This blowgun can be used in a game of competition, much as with darts, by shooting it at a bull's-eye target. See Figure 85.

A bow and arrow set makes a good camp toy, if you can keep the kids from sailing an arrow by your nose while you are cooking by the fire. See Figure 86.

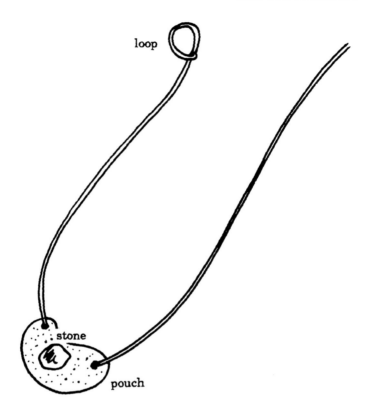

loop

stone

pouch

Figure 84. Sling.

Bamboo or cane is the very best material to use for arrows. Fletching (feathers) is not needed for toy arrows, and the cane material is easily formed into the notch and point. By adding the fletching, you will add to the range of the bow and arrow by 500 or 600 percent, so leave off the fletching for toy use.

For the point of the arrow, cut the cane at an angle. To make an easy string notch, make two cuts from opposite sides of the arrow. This will leave a notch if the arrow is hollow.

The bow can be made from almost any springy limb

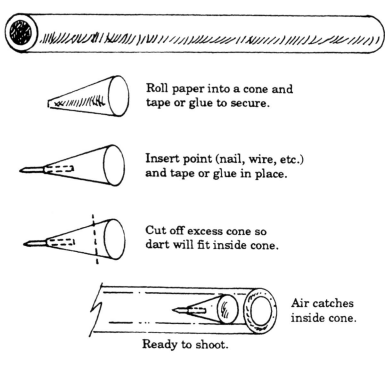

Roll paper into a cone and tape or glue to secure.

Insert point (nail, wire, etc.) and tape or glue in place.

Cut off excess cone so dart will fit inside cone.

Air catches inside cone.

Ready to shoot.

Figure 85. Toy Blowgun.

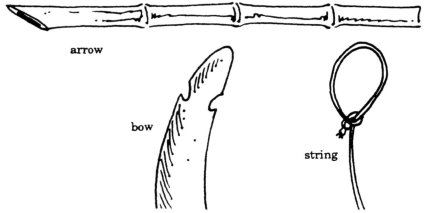

arrow

bow

string

Figure 86. Toy Bow and Arrow.

of appropriate size. A piece of cane or bamboo can be used for the bow as well as the arrows. After all, we are not trying to make a sixty-pound-pull bow, but a toy. Notch each end of the bow to attach the string. Make a loop on each end of the string as shown in Figure 75, and slip each loop into the notches on the bow. Remember to unstring the bow when it is not being used so it will retain its springiness.

CHAPTER FIVE

Path Guarders, Alarms, and Weapons

There may come a time when being able to gather food and secure drinkable water may not be enough to enable you to stay alive. You may have to prevent armed men from entering your territory or, at least, slow them down if they are in pursuit of you and your party. It is hoped that you or I will never have to experience this. But, you never know.

PATH GUARDERS

The devices shown in this section can be very dangerous. Treat them with respect. *Never* set one of these traps except to save your own life. That is the *only* reason they are included in this book. There is always some idiot out there who thinks it might be really "cool" to set one of these for fun. For that reason, I hesitated to include them in this book. Don't be an idiot!

Punji Traps

A path-guarding trap used heavily in Vietnam was

one made of punji sticks in the bottom of a shallow pit, which was covered over to make it appear like solid ground. Punji sticks are simply sharpened pieces of bamboo, although any type of sharpened stick can be used (bamboo was convenient in Vietnam). The sticks were placed in these foot traps with the sharp ends pointing up and the other ends driven into the ground. They were usually dipped in human excrement so that the wounds would become infected. See Figure 87.

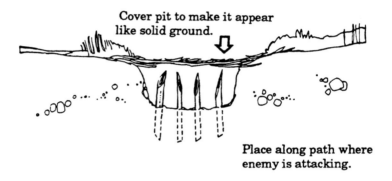

Cover pit to make it appear like solid ground.

Place along path where enemy is attacking.

Figure 87. Punji 1.

After "Charlie" learned that the Vietnam-style boots that American GIs began wearing were at least halfway puncture resistant and had high tops, he started setting the punji traps to work above the boot top.

Figure 88 shows the same basic trap except that the punji sticks face downward at an angle. When you step into the hole, your foot goes down all the way. The normal reaction is to jerk your leg back up. This causes the sharpened spears to puncture the leg *above* the boot top.

Figure 89 shows the same basic trap, except it uses two wood blocks with nails in them which will clamp onto the leg above the boot top as the foot pushes down past the first level of the trap.

Pit is covered to appear solid.

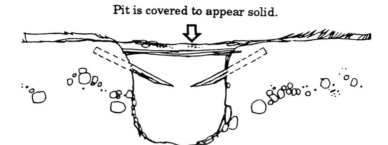

Figure 88. Punji 2.

path of foot

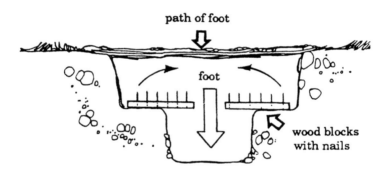

Figure 89. Punji 3.

Bow-and-Arrow Path Guarder

This trap has been seen in a zillion war movies and television shows. It is the ultimate fear inducer, the one that gives you that sick, hollow feeling in the pit of your stomach when you realize you have stepped on the trip line.

The bow-and-arrow path guarder takes a little

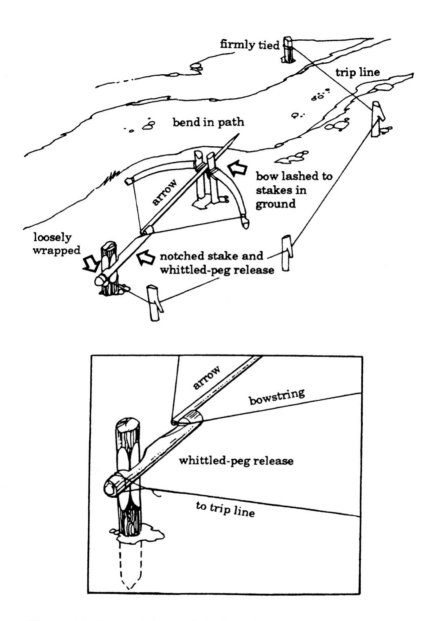

firmly tied

trip line

bend in path

bow lashed to
stakes in
ground

arrow

loosely
wrapped

notched stake and
whittled-peg release

arrow

bowstring

whittled-peg release

to trip line

Figure 90. Bow-and-Arrow Path Guarder.

longer to set than a snare, but the simplicity of the trap is amazing. In actuality, it is somewhat like a snare, but it throws an arrow instead of jerking a snare wire. It does not even matter which direction the victim is walking on the path, because it works both ways.

First, build a bow of whatever strength you feel necessary. Keep in mind when making this bow that the properties of springiness that we discussed earlier in relation to spring poles are essential to this bow as well. Make some arrows out of bamboo, cane, or whatever is available.

Find a bend in the path you wish to guard and set the trap as shown in Figure 90. Examples of arrows are shown in Figure 91. The type of arrow you use depends on the seriousness of your intent and on the materials available.

The damage done to the victim can be heightened or lessened by adjusting the following three factors:

1. *The strength of the bow.* Generally speaking, the harder any particular arrow hits a target, the more damage it will do. As with the spring pole mentioned previously, the strength of the bow can be determined to some degree simply by varying how far back you pull it, as well as the general strength of the materials used. However, this adjustment is not as great with a bow as it is with a spring pole.

2. *The arrow you use.* There may be times when you merely want to scare some trespasser off your land and not hurt anyone, even slightly. In such instances, use the "blank" arrow in Figure 91. Use it in conjunction with a *weak* bow. Even a blank arrow could do damage with a strong enough bow, depending on where it hit. Use just enough bow strength to hurl the arrow toward the trip line—just enough to get the intruder's attention. He is sure to find the bow after the arrow whizzes by. You might even add a note next to the bow that says, "You could've been dead, boy!".

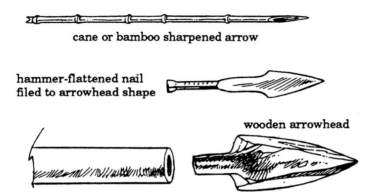

cane or bamboo sharpened arrow

hammer-flattened nail
filed to arrowhead shape

wooden arrowhead

Whittled-wood arrowhead carved to fit in the hollow end of bamboo or cane arrow. Sear the arrowhead in the fire to harden. Use mud to lodge arrowhead firmly in bamboo end.

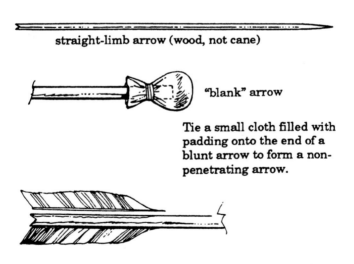

straight-limb arrow (wood, not cane)

"blank" arrow

Tie a small cloth filled with padding onto the end of a blunt arrow to form a non-penetrating arrow.

Fletching: feathers can be glued onto any of these arrow designs if materials are available.

Figure 91. Arrow Details.

3. *The height at which the arrow is aimed.* Obvious reasoning. The chest, stomach, or legs could be your target, depending on your intent. The arrow's elevation is determined by the height at which the bow is lashed to the stakes, the trigger stake height, and the lay of the terrain.

The Stabber

The stabber is another type of path-guarding trap that can be very deadly—or can be set so that, when tripped, it is only a warning to a trespasser of what *could* have happened.

Pick a spot where two trees are growing close together near the path. Cut a springy sapling with the same characteristics as one used for a spring pole. Lash the pole to the two trees so the end of the sapling reaches to at least the center of the path at whatever height is correct for your victim.

Next, lash a sharpened stick or piece of bamboo (or whatever you can scrounge up to use for the stabbing blade) to the end of the stabber arm. Mark the spot below the stabber on the path. This is the point where the trip line will cross the path. Then, bend the pole back as far as you can. Look down and make note of how far you've pulled it back. Three or four feet behind this point will be where you set the trigger. Figures 92 and 93 show the trigger set and the layout of the stabber, respectively.

The damage the stabber does to the victim depends upon the following variables:

1. *The blade.* The length of the blade attached to the stabber arm can obviously make a difference. Also, the number of blades can be increased to four or five along the last two feet of the arm, and the trap can't miss.

It is not imperative, however, to have a blade on the stabber arm. If you have a pesky trespasser that you

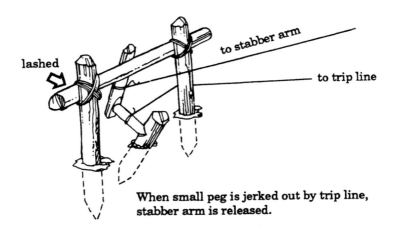

When small peg is jerked out by trip line,
stabber arm is released.

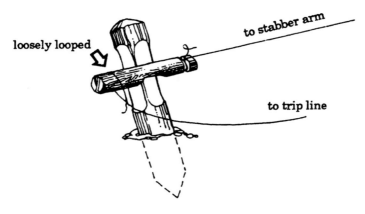

Figure 92. Two Different Trigger Sets.

want to catch in the act, a healthy swat from the
stabber arm about knee level can do wonders even
without a sharp blade. Therefore, the blade variable can
make all the difference in the world, even if the other
variables remain constant.

2. *The pull strength of the stabber arm.* This can
make a difference in the amount of damage done by
whatever you are using on the end of the arm. Even if

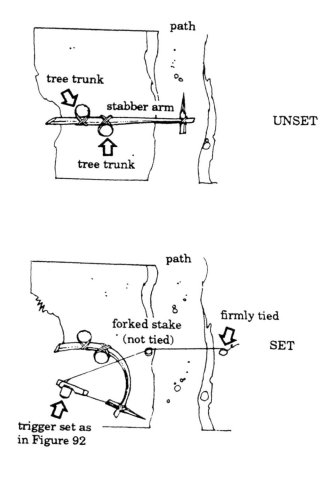

Figure 93.

you use no blade whatsoever, the arm could be so strong it would break a leg, or so weak it would merely swat your victim.

3. *The height of the arm.* Where the arm strikes the victim will make a difference, depending on whether you have set it at a height to catch the vitals or the ankles.

The Foot Snare

The foot snare is another little setup that you see quite a bit in movies. You see a guy walking down a path in the jungle. All of the sudden he is lassoed around the foot, and jerked up into the air upside down.

I do not really care for the foot snare, but I feel it might come in handy in extremely unusual circumstances. I don't like it for several reasons. It's too hard to make and takes too long to set. It's hard to camouflage even in the best of circumstances when you have a lot of brush on the rope side. And, it is basically worthless since there are so many easier methods of slowing someone down.

It is a little less harmful than the stabber and the bow-and-arrow path guarder, but not greatly so. Anytime a person is lassoed around the foot and jerked upside down into the air unexpectedly, he could be seriously hurt. Broken bones, even death, might not be uncommon. So, as with all the dangerous or semi-dangerous traps in this book, never set one except in a struggle to save your life.

The foot snare works very much like the simple snare we have seen earlier except that the snare loop is lying flat on the ground and covered with dirt or leaves, and a trip thread is hung across the center of the loop for the trigger release. See Figure 94.

First, finding the right spot for a foot snare is not always easy. You will almost never be able to use a bent-over sapling as a spring pole for two reasons. First, the sapling would have to be extremely large and strong to be able to pull a man off his feet. If it were that strong, it would take at least two men to set it. Second, it would be nearly impossible to camouflage, and the trap would be readily apparent. So, generally, you must use a weight pull as we did back in Figure 20.

Therefore, in finding a spot you need a *high* limb

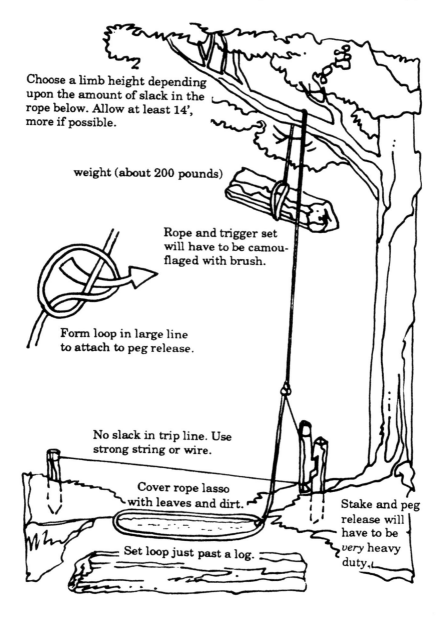

Choose a limb height depending upon the amount of slack in the rope below. Allow at least 14', more if possible.

weight (about 200 pounds)

Rope and trigger set will have to be camouflaged with brush.

Form loop in large line to attach to peg release.

No slack in trip line. Use strong string or wire.

Cover rope lasso with leaves and dirt.

Stake and peg release will have to be *very* heavy duty.

Set loop just past a log.

Figure 94. Foot Snare.

over the intended spot, and brush on the limb side of the path to obscure the rope going up to the limb and over.

For materials, you will need:

1. A rope strong enough to hold two hundred pounds off the ground without breaking. It must be long enough to go from the lasso on the path to the brush beside the path, up to the limb and slightly over the limb to the weight. (Use at least twenty feet, and usually more. See Figure 94 for details.)

2. A weight of some sort, about two hundred pounds. It doesn't matter what the weight is—use a log or whatever is available.

3. A thin cord for the trip line, which will be set in the center of the foot loop. This cord will need to be *very* strong. Fishing line of the heaviest test you can find would be ideal.

4. A big, heavy stake driven in the ground halfway to China for the peg release.

5. A big, heavy whittled-peg release.

6. The patience (and it'll take a lot) to painstakingly camouflage this set so it is not obvious to an enemy coming down the path. See Figures 94, 95, and 96.

If you wish to completely conceal the trip line of the foot snare, dig a small pit where the victim's foot will land after stepping over the log (see Figure 94). Set the trigger as before, except that the trigger line is now stretched at ground level rather than several inches above the ground. In this way the trip line can be concealed with leaves and brush so that the line won't be visible even in daylight. See Figure 95.

A second refinement is to cover the initial trip line with two or more staked lines so that, if the intended victim's foot misses the main trip line and steps on one of the others, the downward pressure created will trip the release anyway. See Figure 96.

•   •   •

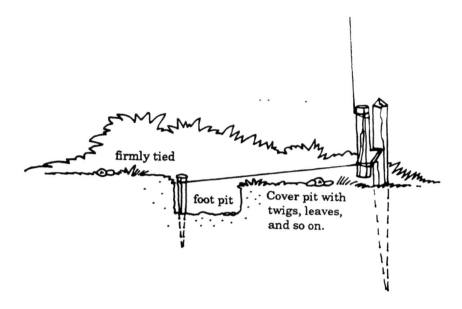

Figure 95. Triggers.

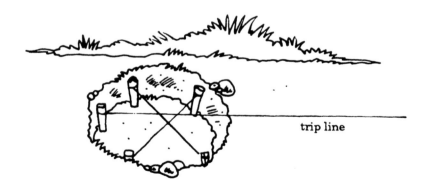

Figure 96.

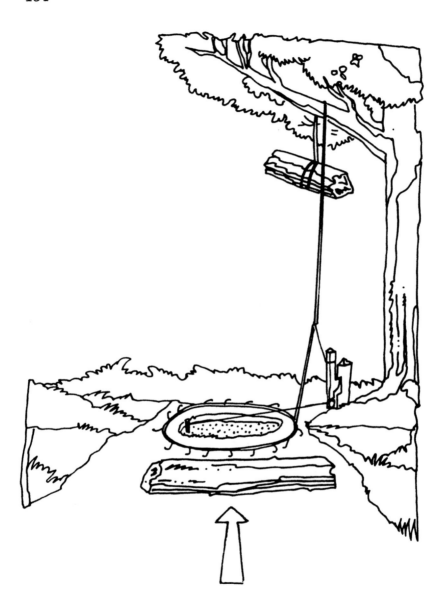

Figure 97. Fishhook Snare.

The next four traps are very similar in nature to the foot snare. The triggers that can be used are identical, and the traps will require little explanation other than the illustrations. For the triggers, look back at Figures 94 and 95. I call these four traps the "fishhook snare," the "fishhook nightmare," the "log jerk," and the "weight slam."

Fishhook Snare

The fishhook snare is a real nasty trap. As with several traps in this chapter, it should never be used except to deter a determined and aggressive enemy. It is simply a foot lasso set up as in Figure 94 except that you (1) make the lasso larger (four feet in diameter or so) so that it will be more likely to catch the victim around both legs, (2) lessen the weight to about twenty pounds or less, and (3) firmly attach a series of fishhooks (or like devices) around the rope lasso. *Note:* These hooks will prevent the lasso from closing up tight when triggered, but the fishhooks will more than make up for this. The purpose of the fishhook snare is to make an aggressor less intense about pursuing you due to several miserable, but probably not fatal, hook wounds. See Figure 97.

Fishhook Nightmare

The fishhook nightmare is an expanded version of the fishhook snare. Use it if you really feel creative. Its advantage is that it can take several victims at once if they are walking down a path single file. Again, the weight is reduced to twenty pounds or less. The object is to slow the enemy down, as he will have to stop to get himself unhooked. See Figure 98.

To make the fishhook nightmare, stake out a series of lines with hooks on the ground across the path. On

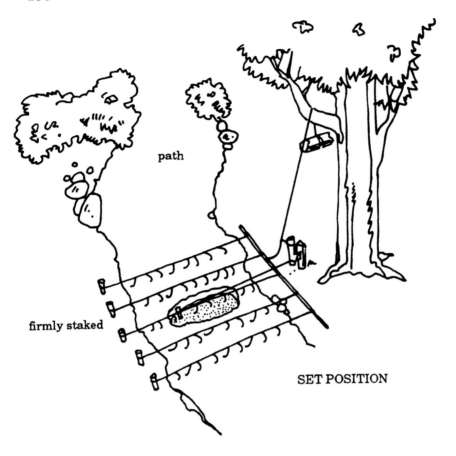

path

firmly staked

SET POSITION

Figure 98. Fishhook Nightmare.

the side away from the stakes, tie each line to a straight
pole. Tie the weighted rope to the center of the pole, and
rig a trigger as shown in Figure 95. Conceal all lines
with dirt and leaves. The pole should be set so that
when tripped, it will go up four feet or so, thus jerking
up the series of hooked lines for several feet along the
path. Barbed wire can be used in place of the hook lines,
but it is harder to camouflage and the barbs are not as
troublesome.

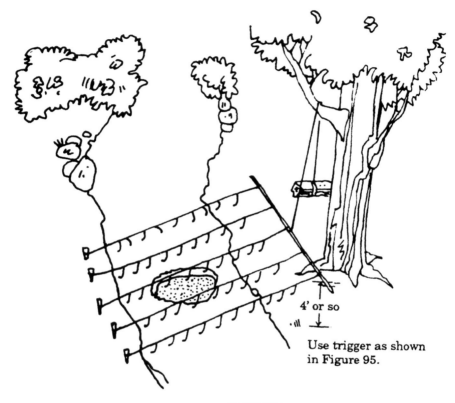

4' or so

Use trigger as shown
in Figure 95.

TRIPPED POSITION

Log Jerk

The log jerk has three features as its main selling
points: (1) it can usually be camouflaged along a path
easily; (2) it tricks the victim into looking one way when
he hears the trip release while he is actually being
attacked from the other side; and (3) it is variable
enough that it can be used to merely swat an intruder,

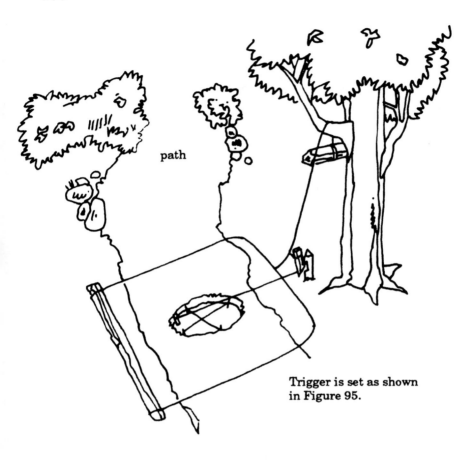

path

Trigger is set as shown
in Figure 95.

Figure 99. Log Jerk.

deal him a crushing blow, or cause even more damage if
blades are inserted in the face of the striking pole. The
effectiveness of this device can be adjusted by varying
the factors discussed earlier for the stabber. You can set
it in a manner consistent with the seriousness of the
threat you face. See Figure 99.

To make the log jerk device, construct the trigger

mechanism as shown in Figure 99. On the opposite side of the path from the whittled-peg release, rig a wood pole, with or without barbs, spikes, or nails on its face. Instead of closing a lasso, this trap will simply cause the wood pole to strike the victim. Unlike some of the other traps in this section, this trap is easy to camouflage along a path.

When the line is tripped, the victim (even if very alert) will naturally look toward the trigger and weight, in the direction from which the sound came. The wood pole will be pulled by the trigger release, and will hit the victim from behind. You can vary the force of the impact by adjusting the amount of weight used and the pole characteristics (heavy, light, with spikes, and so on).

Weight Slam

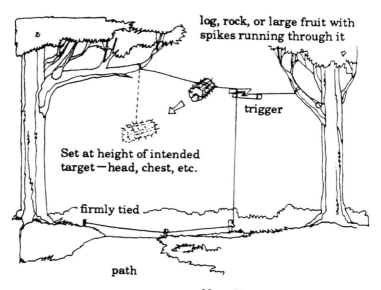

log, rock, or large fruit with spikes running through it

trigger

Set at height of intended target—head, chest, etc.

firmly tied

path

Note: If possible, set the trap so that the weight swings *along* the path rather than across it.

Figure 100. Weight Slam.

The weight slam is another device that can be used as a path guarder. It is simple to construct; see Figure 100 for details.

• • •

The next two path guarders described are land-mine devices. Both utilize a shotgun shell as the detonator. Compared to modern devices, they are primitive, as are most of the traps and devices in this book. However, they will require some advance preparation, and probably could not be built from materials salvaged from a plane crash or a disabled vehicle.

Hotfoot

The "hotfoot" will require one piece of pipe threaded on at least one end, approximately a foot long, and of appropriate inside diameter to accommodate:

1. One shotgun shell (a larger diameter shell, such as a 12-gauge, works better than a smaller shell like a .410).
2. A pipe cap for one end of the pipe.
3. One roofing nail.
4. One piece of wood dowel that fits inside the pipe reasonably tightly but will still slide freely inside.

To make the device, cut off a slice of the dowel about half an inch thick. Drill a hole in the center of it so that the roofing nail will fit into it snugly, but still loose enough that it will slide if bumped. If you get the hole too large for the nail, you can use tree resin or some such material to snug it up in the hole. See Figure 101.

Take the nail out, and glue the dowel slice onto the end of the shell, with the hole you have drilled resting

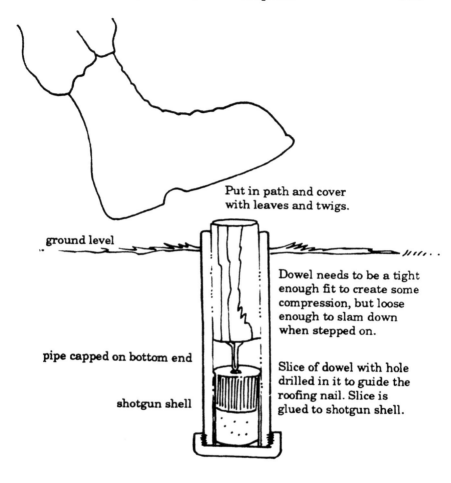

Put in path and cover
with leaves and twigs.

ground level

Dowel needs to be a tight
enough fit to create some
compression, but loose
enough to slam down
when stepped on.

pipe capped on bottom end

Slice of dowel with hole
drilled in it to guide the
roofing nail. Slice is
glued to shotgun shell.

shotgun shell

Figure 101. The Hotfoot.

directly over the firing cap. Insert the nail until it
touches the firing cap.

Cap one end of the pipe firmly and slide the shotgun
shell into the pipe *nail end up.* Bury the pipe in the
ground on the path with the open end above the ground
a quarter of an inch inch or less. Only at this point,

slide the dowel in carefully and slowly until it reaches and rests upon the nail. Then, camouflage the dowel with a leaf or whatever is available. The hotfoot is ready. This device is as safe as anything on this order can be, provided you don't put the dowel in until the final step. See Figure 101.

Second Generation

The "second generation" is very much the same except that the shotgun shell is pointed upward and resting on the detonator nail. The pipe is capped at the top end also with a three-eighths-inch dowel running through a hole in the pipe cap down to the shotgun shell. Shrapnel can be added to the area above the shell, if desired. If so, paper-wrap the shell so it is a reasonably tight fit inside the pipe, thus preventing the shrapnel from sliding past the shell and fouling the nail detonator below.

The second-generation trap has the advantage of greater explosive force than the hotfoot. However, it is more tedious to build. The shell has to be set *precisely* on the nail. To make matters worse, after the shell and nail detonator are in the pipe, the dowel rod has to be inserted, then the shrapnel, then the top cap. Therefore, it is somewhat more dangerous to build and handle. See Figure 102.

Again, don't be stupid. Never set any type of path-guarding trap unless you are out of options and are being pursued by a determined and aggressive enemy. These traps are like the fish bomb described in the fish section: you might be willing to take the slight risk of making the fish bomb if you're starving. If you're not, do something else.

Also, don't overlook the easy stuff, by trying to be exotic. A simple tripping wire staked on both sides is hard to beat, especially at night. The victim trips and

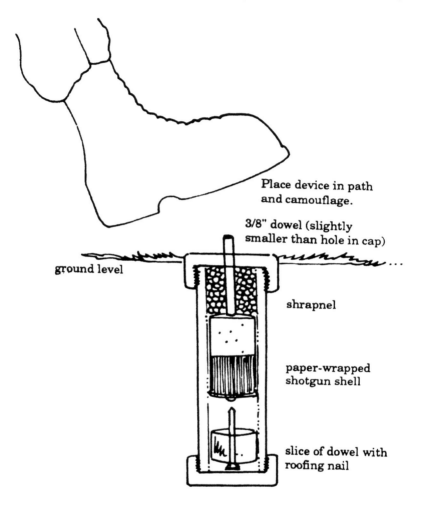

Place device in path
and camouflage.

3/8" dowel (slightly
smaller than hole in cap)

ground level

shrapnel

paper-wrapped
shotgun shell

slice of dowel with
roofing nail

Figure 102. The Second Generation.

falls while walking or running along a path; I will leave
to your discretion what he falls *on*.

ALARMS

At times you can feel more secure at night if the paths into your camp are set with noisemakers to let you know if someone is walking up on you.

Booby-Trap Alarm

The most handy little device I've ever run across is a kind of firework. It is simply a firecracker with a string coming out of each end. When either end is pulled, the firecracker explodes. You do not have to light it with a match or a lighter of any kind, and it is cheap. They are sold under different names, but most people call them "booby traps." At Christmas and other holidays, I stock up. You can buy hundreds of them for two or three dollars.

In case the use of these booby traps is not apparent to you, here is how to use them as a primitive alarm system. Run a string across any likely path into your camp. Tie one end firmly on one side of the path to whatever solid object is available (a tree or stake, for example).

On the other end, tie this string to one of the strings on the booby trap. Tie the string on the other end of the booby trap to something solid on the other side of the path. Set the string across the path so it is about one foot from the ground and fairly taut. See Figure 103.

When someone comes down the path during the night, his foot will catch on the string, jerking it and exploding the firecracker. If one of these booby traps is not loud enough, tie six or eight of them together in the same fashion. The more, the merrier!

These booby traps will have to be bought, as opposed to being homemade as are most of the things in this book. I suspect that they may be difficult to make yourself, and they are cheap, so why bother? Buy some

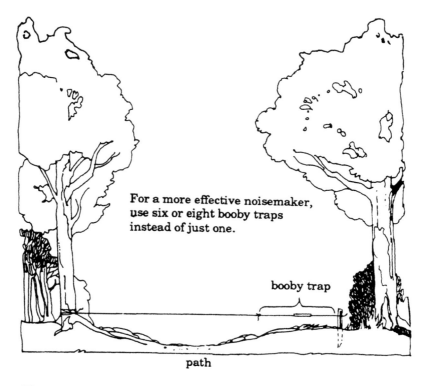

For a more effective noisemaker, use six or eight booby traps instead of just one.

booby trap

path

Figure 103. Booby-Trap Alarm.

soon, since they might not be available when you actually need them.

There is an added benefit to these alarms. In addition to letting you know of an intruder, they are great for scaring off the weak at heart. A would-be bad guy coming into your camp for no good reason would likely have second thoughts if a dozen firecrackers explode close by in the dark when he trips the trip wire.

Tin-Can Snare

An alarm I like a lot is the tin-can snare. It is very much like a simple snare except that it jerks up (or

wired-up bundle of tin cans

The trigger is loosely
attached in notch cut in peg.

firmly tied

path

Figure 104. Tin-Can Snare.

drops) a wired-up bundle of about twenty tin cans, making a heck of a racket.

Set a stake in the ground with a nail in it, and rig a whittled-peg release. Run the cord over a limb and tie it to about twenty cans instead of running it to a spring pole. String a trip line across the path and attach the string loosely to the whittled peg. *Loosely* is the key word in the last sentence. See Figure 104.

When the trip line is tripped, the cans will fall with a loud racket. You can even have them fall on your intruder if there is a convenient limb available. For that matter, if the situation were desperate enough, you could drop something other than tin cans on him. That will be left to your discretion.

You can reverse the procedure if you wish. Instead of the tin cans dangling in the air as in Figure 104, put a weight in their place. Then, on the ground, tie the coil of tin cans to the whittled-peg release so that when the wire is tripped, the cans go up, rattling all the way.

Shotgun-Shell Alarm

Another great alarm for a path into your area makes use of a shotgun shell. First, since this is just an alarm, open the end of the shell and take out the pellets. (Yes, I know it makes a good claymore if you don't, and I know that you can set them in paths for people to step on, but this is only a scare-type alarm.)

A trip line is set to a release peg as we have done many times so far. The line from the release peg is run over a limb and down to a weight. Make sure the weight is suspended so that it will hit the shell solidly. If necessary, place a small log across the top of the shell for a larger target. When tripped, the weight falling will strike the shotgun shell poised on a nail (detailed in Figure 105), detonating it. This creates one heck of a

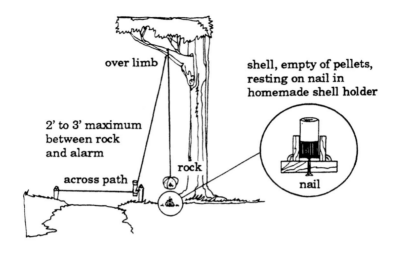

over limb

shell, empty of pellets,
resting on nail in
homemade shell holder

2' to 3' maximum
between rock
and alarm

across path

rock

nail

Figure 105. Shotgun-Shell Alarm.

noise. A weak heart will flutter when one of these goes off a few feet away. See Figure 105.

Mousetrap Shooter

The next alarm is called a "mousetrap shooter." It is a monumental amount of trouble to build, but when triggered at night, it creates a scary, surprising visual effect on the victim. When the trip line is touched (or breathed on, almost, in this case), it fires a series of bottle rockets at the victim. In the dark, it is possible that this could have enough of a surprising effect that an intruder might have to change wardrobe. It's loads of fun!

You will need the following materials: a small amount of gunpowder, a piece of plastic pipe capped on one end, a flashlight bulb (or something similar), some electrical wire, a mousetrap (or similar trigger—see variations), a battery, about ten bottle rockets, and the usual trip-line setup.

The principle behind this device is simple. Did you ever, as a kid, take a piece of cardboard and stick a Coke bottle through the center of it, and then put in about ten bottle rockets, and light *one* of them? When the first bottle rocket takes off, spewing out of the bottle, it lights the fuses on some of the others, and so it goes until all of the rockets are fired. The first couple take a second or two but, after that, it seems as if they go off like a machine gun. The cardboard's function is to protect you from the spewing sparks, allowing you to hold the back of the bottle and *aim* it in the desired direction. The general principle of the mousetrap shooter is the same. The difference is that you are rigging it to go off all by itself.

With materials at hand, first break the flashlight bulb without breaking the filament. This is not easy. It may take two or three bulbs to accomplish this feat.

Then solder two pieces of electrical wire to the contact points on the bulb. You may find it easier to do the soldering before you break the glass on the bulb.

The bulb, with wires attached, is inserted into the bottom of the plastic pipe and covered with the powder. The wires soldered to the bulb's contact points run out the open end of the pipe.

Lodge the pipe securely in an appropriate location pointing at the trip line. Insert the bottle rockets, breaking off the sticks if they are too long. Attach the wires to the battery/trigger assembly shown in the illustration. What happens is this: when the trip wire is merely *touched*, it snaps the mousetrap, thus completing the electrical circuit. This current then passes through the filament in the powder. The powder flashes, setting off some of the bottle rockets instantly, the others within a few seconds. If you use about ten bottle

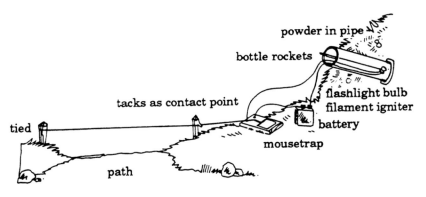

Figure 106. Mousetrap Shooter.

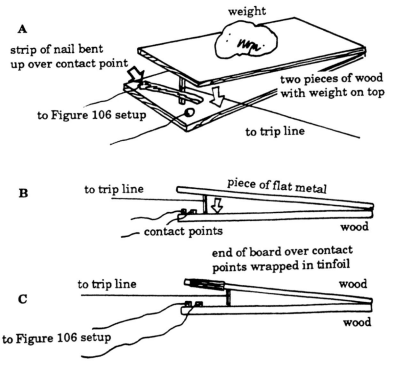

Figure 107. Alternate Triggers.

rockets, usually at least seven or eight will fire. The visual effect on the unsuspecting is not for the weak at heart. In the dark, they may even think it is tracer shells coming at them. See Figures 106 and 107.

•   •   •

All these little alarms will alert you to the presence of an intruder. They are all shown constructed in such a way that they would not be lethal, barring some accident. Obviously, the mousetrap shooter and the shotgun-shell alarm could be constructed in such a way as to be very dangerous, but that is another story. As alarms, these devices will at least let you know something is coming.

WEAPONS

There are many things that could be discussed in the realm of weapons, but this section is centered around ideas for a few items that might help in a general survival situation. Also, some of these primitive weapons might slow down a pursuing human adversary long enough for you to get away. This is not a section on "fight-back" weapons, but a "slow 'em down and run like the devil" section.

Staff

For traveling cross-country, as well as around the camp, a good walking stick or staff is hard to beat. The following one is a combination club, spear, walking staff, wood gatherer, and latrine.

Its uses are many. As a weapon, it can be used as a club, fighting staff, spear, or lance. It would be useful in dealing with small animals such as biting dogs or

about 1" diameter hardwood

about 5' to 6' long

Figure 108. Staff.

snakes. As a tool, it is a good gatherer of dry firewood lodged in brush or trees due to the hook on the end of the staff. As a walking staff, it is also good for an improvised commode seat when lodged between two objects horizontally at appropriate height. Also, if the staff is made at home ahead of time, the blunt end could be drilled out and reserve matches could be corked inside for emergencies.

If you have to cut your staff on the spot in the forest, find a sapling of reasonably uniform diameter (about one inch) and five to six feet long. Cut it off so that one of the limbs forms a barb as shown. Hardwood would be good for this. Don't use a gummy softwood. See Figure 108.

Bow and Arrows

Some time ago, I became interested in the construction of archery equipment from primitive materials. Having a modern compound bow and some limited experience at deer hunting (the deer population in my area probably doesn't feel all that threatened), I figured that constructing these primitive bows and arrows like the Indians did was going to be very difficult.

After many trials and errors over a long period of time, I decided I was right. I would have been a miserable Indian. The toy bow and arrow, described in Chapter Four, is easy to make. But making a bow to use as a hunting or antipersonnel weapon is quite a chore.

Once made, however, a bow and arrows do make a good delivery system as a makeshift grenade launcher, even if you do not use them for hunting. After the construction details, we will get into such uses in the arrow section.

First, the bow itself. Finding the right kind of sapling or limb is not easy. Find a piece of wood about five feet long, which is about right for most average-size men. Try to find a piece of wood that is no larger than about an inch in diameter, because anything larger would be too difficult to hold and shoot. One end will almost always be slightly larger than the other—this is fine. A *slight* curve is okay, but not mandatory.

After locating the wood of suitable size, test it for springiness. This springiness is what we looked for in a spring pole in the snare section. It can't be a wood species that is so stiff it won't bend. On the other hand, it can't be a wood that has a weak spring-back action or a wood that will bend but quickly lose its tendency to spring back when released. You can test this by bending it a few times. If it doesn't pop back smartly to its original shape, it won't do.

Take your time. A pole with the above features simply won't be found without a *lot* of looking. The particular species of wood that will be good for bow making will vary from area to area. In your area, you may find a dry, dead piece of wood with these features, or it might be a green wood. It usually takes a lot of looking.

Once the wood is selected, notch each end for the bow string exactly as we did earlier in the toy section. Refer to Figure 86 if necessary. Tie a loop on both ends of a string of appropriate length and size. Bend the bow and attach the string.

Five notes about the bow:

1. Try to scrounge up a string or cord (or even wire, though string is much better) for the bow string. Animal tendon like the Indians used is hard to come by and vines are almost impossible to use in this fashion. *Heavy* trotline cord is ideal.

2. In selecting the material for the bow, quite often you will find a piece of limb with a secondary small limb on one end that makes a small fork at the end it of the bow. If you find such a piece, you can loop the string on

the main beam, using the smaller limb as a stop. By doing this, you will only have to notch out the other end for the string, not both ends.

3. Unstring the bow when not in use. This preserves the springiness.

4. Make an extra string in case you break one.

5. To have any hope that your bow will be strong enough to hunt with, it will have to be of such strength that it is a definite strain to draw back. If you are able to hold the bow at full draw for more than a few seconds, it is not strong enough.

Cane or bamboo is the best wood for primitive arrows I have come across, for several reasons. First of all, in a cane patch, you can always find a large amount of *straight* cane to use. To test this relative straightness, cut a three-foot section that looks straight and hold it at the end, eyeing it like a telescope.

Second, cane is easy to notch for the string. Two knife cuts form a notch if made from opposing sides of the arrow. Also, cane is very easy to add fletching to, using vines, feathers, and so on. The fact that fletching is imperative can easily be proven by shooting the same arrow with and without fletching. The same arrow won't go far or straight if the fletching is taken off. Fletching is *essential*. Also, the point end of a cane arrow is easy to sharpen, and adding arrowheads is relatively simple.

If you cannot find cane or bamboo, and have to use a solid arrow, you will have to glue on the fletching or split the end of the arrow, insert the fletching, bind the end back, and then make the notch. The bow and arrow also can be used as a primitive grenade launcher, which will be shown in illustration form. See Figures 109, 110, 111, and 112.

Figure 113 shows an improvised grenade-launcher arrow. The detonator is a slice of dowel, with a hole drilled into the center, glued onto the end of a shotgun

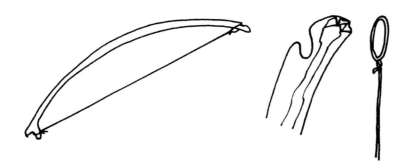

Figure 109. The Bow.

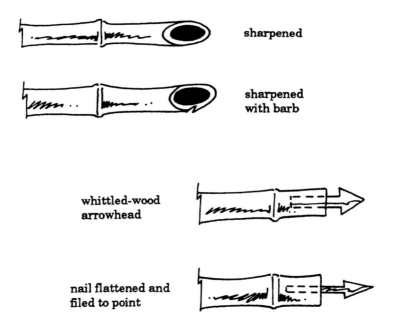

Figure 110. Cane Arrow Points.

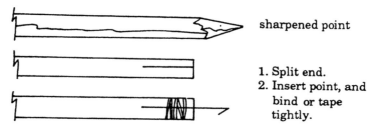

sharpened point

1. Split end.
2. Insert point, and
   bind or tape
   tightly.

Figure 111. Solid Arrow Points.

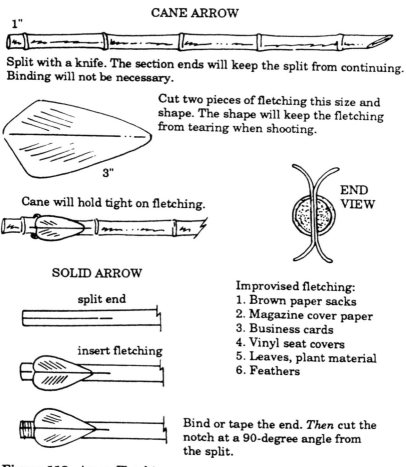

CANE ARROW

1"

Split with a knife. The section ends will keep the split from continuing.
Binding will not be necessary.

Cut two pieces of fletching this size and
shape. The shape will keep the fletching
from tearing when shooting.

3"

Cane will hold tight on fletching.

END
VIEW

SOLID ARROW

split end

insert fletching

Improvised fletching:
1. Brown paper sacks
2. Magazine cover paper
3. Business cards
4. Vinyl seat covers
5. Leaves, plant material
6. Feathers

Bind or tape the end. *Then* cut the
notch at a 90-degree angle from
the split.

Figure 112. Arrow Fletching.

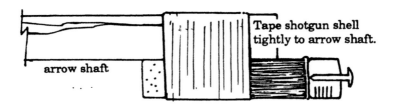

Tape shotgun shell tightly to arrow shaft.

arrow shaft

Figure 113. Grenade Launcher.

shell. A roofing nail is inserted so that when the arrow strikes the ground or the victim, the shell will detonate. Getting the proper amount of extra weight at the point will require some practice. Though the shell going off will by no means be like a bomb, it might slow down a pursuer long enough for you to escape.

The actual utility of the primitive bow and arrow depends not only on the quality and strength of the equipment, but on the general conditions at the time. This will apply to its use as a hunting weapon or a combat weapon.

In hunting, the amount of game in the area you are stranded in will obviously make a difference. For example, if you are in an area that is *teeming* with deer, and you can sit patiently (and camouflaged) beside a deer trail in wait, you *might* have some luck. But there better be enough deer in the area so you are practically stumbling over them. At best, even if you constructed an *extremely strong* bow and had good arrows, you wouldn't down a large animal like a deer instantly. They don't just drop as is shown on TV. Maybe with a modern bow and razor-sharp arrows, but not with this primitive equipment. On a large animal, you might have to follow it for a day or two before it succumbs. Large game is one heck of a challenge with modern archery equipment, and is even more difficult if you use primitive equipment.

In another, easier scenario, I have been in river bottoms that have enormous populations of squirrels. If you sat still, you could watch literally hundreds of them running around. You'll miss nine out of ten due to the limited accuracy of this primitive equipment, but you may have some luck in such a situation. The blowgun described in the toy section of this book may be useful for small squirrels and birds. Refer to that section.

Rabbits can also be taken with this equipment in an area where they are abundant. I have walked to within a few feet of rabbits in the woods many times. Again, you'll miss a lot, but not every time.

In the desperation category, slow, ground-dwelling animals like armadillos can be taken with this equipment. Most people would have to be near starving to cook an armadillo, but who knows?

The best use of the bow and arrow for food gathering may be in fishing. If you are near water shallow enough that you can see fish swimming, but do not have any fishing equipment, you may have some luck with the bow and arrow.

As a combat weapon, the bow and arrow can be limited by many factors: how well armed your pursuers are, how close they are, how strong your equipment is, how professional your enemy is, the terrain, and so on. There are two main uses for the bow and arrow in a combat situation. Both deal more with getting away than with defeating an adversary.

First, if an enemy is in close pursuit and some cover for yourself is available, an arrow fired within a few feet of most people would slow them down and make them considerably more cautious in their pursuit. This may allow you to get away. Of course, if you manage to hit the aggressor, it will slow him down even more. But, even if you miss, an arrow slamming hard into a tree a few feet away will make you less desirable as a prey in most cases.

Second, the primitive grenade launcher (as shown in Figure 113) can be used for much the same purpose: to scare off an adversary and allow you to escape.

Arrow Shooter

Another bow-and-arrow type weapon that is good for hunting small animals and for sailing arrows past a pursuer's head is a device I call an "arrow shooter." It is simply a slingshot that shoots an arrow rather than a pellet or a rock.

I started thinking about this weapon several years ago when deer hunting. After reaching my hunting stand, I had trouble with dogs coming through the area, barking, chasing rabbits, and generally messing up the morning's deer hunting. I wanted to get rid of them, but didn't want to shoot them with a big-bore deer rifle because of the noise. I began with an idea that a slingshot weapon could be made that would shoot a small, short arrow very hard, fast, and accurately.

Off and on, over the next several months, I toyed with various ideas about how to make it. I discovered that you can't hold it like a slingshot. If you do, you can't pull it back far enough to shoot more than a few feet because the wrist of the hand holding the handle will give way.

What developed after much experimentation was this: you need a typical forked stick like any slingshot, except the bottom of the stick needs to be about three feet long with at least a rounded point on the bottom, if not a sharp point. See Figure 114.

For the elastic, you need eight or ten rubber bands on each side. By rubber bands, I mean those *big heavy* rubber bands that are about three-eighths of an inch wide that are used to bind big bundles of mail, for example, *not* the little ones you might have in your desk drawer or around a newspaper.

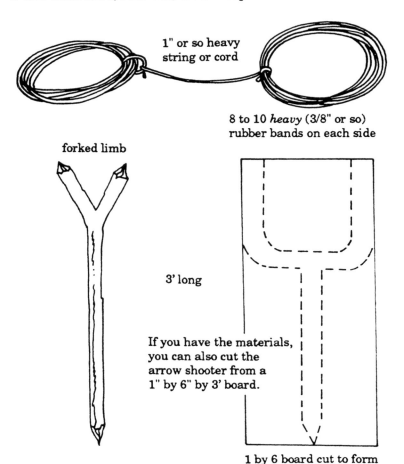

1" or so heavy string or cord

8 to 10 *heavy* (3/8" or so) rubber bands on each side

forked limb

3' long

If you have the materials, you can also cut the arrow shooter from a 1" by 6" by 3' board.

1 by 6 board cut to form

Figure 114. Materials for Arrow Shooter.

Attach a one-inch or so piece of heavy cord in between the rubber bands that you attach to each fork. This is where the arrow catches.

The arrows for this device have to be very exact. The best size is about three-eighths of an inch in diameter and ten to twelve inches long. I used three-eighths-inch wood dowels in constructing the ones I made. You cut a notch in the front end of the arrow and put fletching on

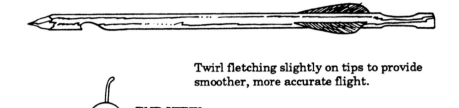

Twirl fletching slightly on tips to provide smoother, more accurate flight.

END VIEW

Figure 115. Arrow-Shooter Arrows.

the back end. You can use black electrical tape for fletching; stick it onto the shaft and cut it to the appropriate shape. It is very sturdy. Cut two notches in the back end behind the fletching for "finger holders," which allow you to pull the arrow back farther. Use solid wood for these arrows, not cane. See Figure 115.

To shoot, drop down to one knee and stick the sharp end of the stick in the ground. Then, catch the arrow notch on the string, pull back, and fire. The power generated by this arrow shooter is hard to believe. It will fire an arrow at great velocity for a hundred and fifty yards *easily*, and probably a lot farther with a little refinement of the building technique or a stronger elastic. *Helpful hint:* Use a glove on the pull-back hand to increase the power, speed, and distance of arrow flight.

The arrow shooter is very accurate. Hitting a human-size target at one hundred yards, though difficult, would not be impossible with this device. Sailing an arrow within a few feet of the target at the same distance would be child's play. The speed and straight flight of these arrows is difficult to believe, considering you are doing this with rubber bands. Sounds absurd, doesn't it? But, it works.

It could be there is a better commercial grade of this item on the market. I've never seen anything like it in a store, but it seems inconceivable to me that no one else has thought of it. I'm sure someone has probably marketed an item like this at one time or another—perhaps a better one. But the arrow shooter is so easy to make, why buy one? See Figures 114 and 115.

Band Bow

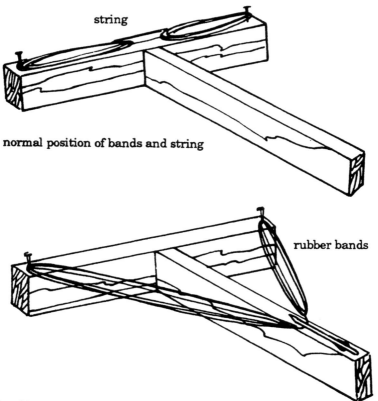

Band bow is in ready-to-fire position. The string is pulled back and the bands are stretched; the arrow is nocked with the string in the notch on the *underside* of the arrow.

Figure 116. Band Bow.

The band bow is a variation of the technique used in the arrow shooter. For the bow, you nail two two-by-fours together at a right angle to form a "T." The leg of the T should be about three feet long and the horizontal bar should be about two feet. Drive a nail in each end of the crossbar, letting them stick out about two inches. These need to be nails with a head on them (common nails), not headless nails (such as casing nails). Attach to these nails the same band/string arrangement as used for the arrow shooter. Their own elastic pull will keep them in place without having to tie them to the nails. See Figure 116.

The weight of the two-by-fours is not excessive, and it allows for stabilization in aiming without having to plant the end in the ground, as with the arrow shooter. It uses the same arrows and the same general technique as the arrow shooter. It is possible to rig an actual trigger, crossbow fashion, on the band bow. Use the notch on the back of the arrow to catch the rubber band and string, as shown in Figure 116. Finally, by sitting on the ground and looping the elastic bands on your feet (spread about a foot apart), you can use this system without any wood supports.

AFTERWORD

Into the Primitive deals with making do with what you have. More than any specific item or technique, this book presents a way of thinking about obstacles and how they can be overcome.

I hope that you or I will never have to endure the hardships that would force us to use the trapping and food-gathering techniques described in this book. It is hoped that we will all live to a ripe old age in our comfortable homes, and will never find ourselves stranded in a remote wilderness. But, you never know. Enjoy!